# Qualitative Research
## Tips, Tricks, and Trends

# Qualitative Research
# Tips, Tricks, and Trends

## What Every Researcher Should Know

**Mary Kathryn Malone**
Appleseed Consumer Insight

Illustrated by
Mike Thomas, Creative Giant

Paramount Market Publishing, Inc.

Paramount Market Publishing, Inc.
950 Danby Road, Suite 136
Ithaca, NY 14850
www.paramountbooks.com
Telephone: 607-275-8100; 888-787-8100    Facsimile: 607-275-8101

Publisher: James Madden
Editorial Director: Doris Walsh
Copyright © 2011 Mary Kathryn Malone
Printed in USA

*Appleseed Consumer Insight is a tradename of Mary Kathryn Malone*

Cataloging in Publication Data available
ISBN-10: 0-9819869-9-4  |  ISBN-13: 978-0-9819869-9-9

# Contents

# Preface

JUDGING by the fact that you are reading this, you are interested in learning more about qualitative research (or you got this book for Christmas . . . from me). Either way, the next several chapters are packed full of ideas you can use to get started, to improve, or to rethink your approach to qualitative research. This is a practical book, not a theoretical book. Books on research theory abound, and if that is your interest, this will fall short. But if you want tips, tricks, and ideas, this is the book for you.

Maybe you do only a few projects every year and are looking for tips; maybe you do many projects every year and are looking for ways to amp it up. Either way, this book will give you food for thought and some trade tricks to make your projects shine.

The focus here is on qualitative research—interviewing people, having a dialogue. This book does *not* deal with large sample size studies or online quantitative surveys, or projects where you poll people about which mayoral candidate they might vote for or what flavor of ice cream they want.

It is about the critical conversations we should have with people, one at a time, in a group, by phone, in person, just about anywhere and which, when done effectively, will make your business, your brand, your product better. It is about the tools and tricks you can use to get beyond yes and no answers to insights and understanding. Only by getting creative and listening with open ears and viewing with open eyes can you really start to know your consumer, your prospect, or your constituent.

This book comes to you with input gathered from more than 50 marketing research executives, practitioners, and suppliers working in the field every day. These people generously participated in the 2010 Appleseed Survey of Researchers. It is also drawn from my own personal time in the trenches—close to 20 years' worth.

In researching the book it was clear there are some fundamental questions that require a 360-degree look at the field. Some of the questions I hope to answer in the next several chapters include:

How can some of the most common pitfalls in qualitative be avoided?

What do clients want that they are not getting?

How can research be more engaging and inspirational?

What is the best way to get to "insights" and report them?

What are the trends in qualitative and how can they help me?

How has technology changed the way qualitative research is done?

This is just the beginning of the conversation. It continues at *www.appleseedconsumerinsight.com*. Share your thoughts and tips and see what others are saying. If you like the pictures and graphs in this book, check out *www.creativeGIANT.com*. A better artist and creative mind than Mike Thomas you will not find, I promise you.

Happy Researching!

# Acknowledgments

AS I BEGAN the research and writing process, it struck me that this task was not going to be a one-person endeavor. I owe a debt of gratitude to the many exceptional people in my life and to those I met along the journey. I would like to take a moment here to acknowledge some of them formally and permanently in print.

Thanks to my marketing research colleagues and friends for their professional guidance and personal support throughout the writing and editing process. First to my great friend Michelle Monkoski who keeps my head on straight, to Heather Tullio who is as good a sounding board as anyone you will ever find, and to Suchi Patel and Tara Scholder who provided a sharp perspective and keen edit and without whom the book would have been only half baked. Thanks to Patricia Hussong for her many hours of proofreading. And to everyone who said I wasn't crazy, and even those who did, thank you.

Special thanks go to Kate Albert of Fieldwork, Inc., and Dan Cotter of Suburban Focus Group – Boston. Both of these exceptional researchers generously shared their perspective on the facility side of the qualitative research business.

This book also comes with thanks due to the many, many nameless people out there who took time from their day to answer the 2010 Appleseed Survey of Researchers. All of us in research know that we owe our professional success to people like this— people who are willing to share time and information in the interest of research.

Thanks to the A.C. Nielsen Center for Marketing Research at the University of Wisconsin, Madison, first for the educational grounding it provided, second for the eternal support I receive, and finally for their assistance in the execution of the 2010 Survey of Researchers. If you seek the best in a market research education, you owe it to yourself to check out this master's program.

And a very personal note of thanks to my family and to the Lang family for the many hours of puppy-sitting and more home-cooked meals than I can count as I tried to balance writing with working. You are my heroes. I could not be me without you.

Finally, thanks to Anne Marie Weiss. You know what you did.

# SECTION 1

# Getting the Room Just Right

GROUP A          GROUP B

# CHAPTER 1

# Recruiting Dos and Definite Don'ts

THE FIRST hurdle any qualitative researcher has to overcome is getting the right people to talk with about the subject of interest. This is no small feat, and even with the growth in consumer panels and the online tools that manage them, finding and retaining qualified participants is still one of the biggest challenges the market research industry faces. The next several chapters deal exclusively with this topic.

This is an ad that appeared on craigslist in a Southern city. Its headline was "Conservatives Needed for Focus Group." The ad continues:

A local law firm is having two focus groups on Thursday, June 24. Compensation is $55 for four hours of participation, including $5 for parking and free food and beverages during the event. There will be two sessions, each requiring different participants. The AM session will run from 8:45 a.m.–1:05 p.m. and the PM session will run from 1:45 p.m. to 6:05 p.m. When completing your questionnaire, please indicate if you prefer the AM or PM session, or if you do not have a preference which time you participate. Please note that the presenters are looking for politically conservative people to participate and keep in mind that incomplete applications will not be considered. Participants will be notified if they have been selected by June 21.

Besides basic questions on contact information, session preferences, gender, age, and race, the applicant must also respond to the following questions:

When it comes to politics, please select the answer that best describes you:

- a. Very liberal
- b. Somewhat liberal
- c. Middle of the road
- d. Somewhat conservative
- e. Very conservative

For each of the following names, please indicate how you feel about the person by assigning them a corresponding letter:
a. Really like; b. Like; c. Neutral; d. Dislike; e. Really dislike:

1. Sarah Palin
2. Barack Obama
3. George W. Bush
4. Bill Clinton
5. Nancy Pelosi
6. Hillary Clinton

---

This ad is riddled with issues. First, it specifically describes the respondent's preferred political ideology. Second, the qualifying questions are given right on the page and the answers are not very subtle, to say the least. If you wanted to be in this group and earn a few bucks, it is not a hard screener to "pass." This violates the first cardinal rule of research: Don't give respondents any incentive to cheat!

Here is another example from craigslist in a Northeastern market, in April 2010. This is copied verbatim from the ad.

## Recruiting ad

We have an amazing new real estate concept and want to get feedback from some real estate agents. We'll pay you $50 to sit in a one-hour focus group in Dorchester, MA. We'll keep the focus group to 1 hour of your time. To qualify, you must be a licensed real estate agent and have done at least 6 transactions in the prior 24 months.

The event will be held on April 22, 2010 at Philips Old Colony House–Dorchester at 12:00PM (Doors open from 11:45AM and close after 12:05PM). You will be provided a three-course meal during the focus group and you will be able to choose from steak, chicken or vegetarian for your entrée. No obligations other than give us your honest feedback. You get paid immediately after the focus group. Each focus group is limited to just 20 participants. We also have upcoming focus groups in Westboro & Quincy.

Here are just some of the reasons why you should be unhappy if this group was being recruited for you:

- First, the ad essentially feeds interested people answers to the questions—namely that you must have done six real estate transactions in the last two years. If you want an honest recruit, why would you advertise what you are looking for? This is gilding the lily and you should never do this or allow it to be done.

- Second, the ad leads with the incentive. If you want to earn $50 and have a nice meal you might be more inclined to lie. Granted, $50 for two hours is not a high incentive, but still.

- Third, the location, time and date are listed. Why invite crashers to your research? This information should only be shared with qualified recruits.

- Finally, it is unlikely they will get honest feedback about the new idea because they have already positioned it as an "amazing" new concept. It seems like they are serving bias along with the three-course meal!

Ads like this appear everyday around the country, and not just on craigslist. They appear in newspapers in the help wanted section, on or in websites devoted to connecting people with research groups, and myriad other portals designed to get people signed up for research projects and into focus-group databases. While casting these wide nets is not a major issue, and is often done to recruit panelists, it can be a problem when you see how these "nets" are cast as in these examples.

However, all is not lost. Below is an example of a good craigslist posting. This ad does not disclose the study details, the incentive, or the location. You are more likely to get an "authentic" respondent with this approach:

We are a national market research company specializing in automotive research seeking participants for upcoming paid focus groups. To be considered, please provide the following information. A member of our recruiting team will contact you if you meet our desired profile. Thank you.

Name

Age

Town/City

Marital status

Any children under age 18 reside in household?
    If so, please list ages and gender

Occupation

Household Vehicle(s)
    If yes, please include year/make/model of each vehicle

Cell phone owned? If yes, please include manufacturer of phone

Other mobile device(s) owned?

　　If yes, please include manufacturer of each item

Child's car seats owned? If yes, please include manufacturer

Not convinced that this level of caution is really necessary? In June 2004, Will Leitch, a writer and editor in New York wrote an article exposing the ease of "cheating" in research and the profitable reasons someone might want to engage in such behavior. In the article he describes his first-hand experience gaming the system and offers hints for others to do the same. For example, "If they ask you something off-the-wall, like 'Have you purchased a treadmill in the last year?' say yes." After all, he says, "They wouldn't ask if that weren't the answer they wanted." He goes on to talk about how to behave once you are in the group. His advice, "be as invisible as possible." Otherwise you will be tagged as an outlier and might not be invited into future research. This article appeared in *New York* magazine years ago but lives forever on the Internet. If you are in research, this is your worst nightmare. (*http://nymag.com/nymetro/shopping/features/9299/*)

Anecdotes like Leitch's are not uncommon in qualitative research. You could ask just about any qualitative research consultant, and he or she would likely have plenty of stories from the road. The point is you need to be on guard for this type of scammer and take appropriate steps to keep your study real.

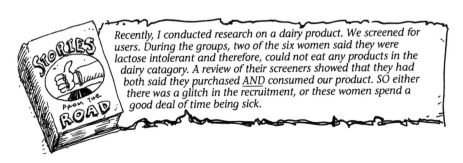

Recently, I conducted research on a dairy product. We screened for users. During the groups, two of the six women said they were lactose intolerant and therefore, could not eat any products in the dairy catagory. A review of their screeners showed that they had both said they purchased AND consumed our product. SO either there was a glitch in the recruitment, or these women spend a good deal of time being sick.

Don't be fooled into thinking that it is just respondents who are trying to game the system; there are issues on the recruiter side as well. In our 2010 Appleseed Survey of Researchers, three in four respondents said that improvement was needed in recruiting.

Along with what we saw in the Appleseed Survey, this problem is documented in the following transcript of an actual interview between Jim Schwartz and a recruiter. Here is an edited version that appeared in the April 1992 issue of *Quirk's Marketing Research Review.*

REC refers to the recruiter. JS refers to the respondent, Jim Schwartz, who wrote the article.

REC: Please tell me how many days in the last 12 months you have stayed at hotels in each of the following chains. Hotel A?

JS: Three.

REC: Hotel B?

JS: Six.

REC: Hotel C?

JS: None.

REC: Hotel D?

JS: Two.

REC: Hotel E?

JS: None.

REC: Hotel F?

JS: None.

REC: Try and think about Hotel F again. Can you stretch your answer to "at least twice" in the last twelve months? Try and stretch.

*Comment:* This is quite remarkable. She is now asking me to lie. She must be desperate to recruit people. All right, I'll accommodate her.

JS: If you want me to say "two," I'll say "two."

REC: Good. Now, please tell me how many different hotels in

each of these chains you have stayed at during the last 12 months. Hotel A?

JS: One.

REC: Hotel B?

JS: One.

REC: Hotel C?

JS: None.

REC: Hotel D?

JS: One.

REC: Hotel E?

JS: None.

REC: Hotel F?

JS: Is "none" OK?

REC: No. Try and stretch. Try and think if you have stayed in at least two different Hotel F hotels in the past 12 months.

JS: OK. If that is what you want (I'll lie for you), two.

REC: If you had an eleven-day trip to schedule, please tell me how many days you would stay at each of these chains.

JS: (Let me see if she will spill her beans here.) Does this question matter?

REC: No, it doesn't. Can I help you with this? Let's mark down six for Hotel B, three for Hotel E, two for Hotel A, and zero for the others.

REC: OK, that completes the interview. You will get a card in the mail confirming the date, time and with directions. Let me confirm your address, etc.

---

Stories like this are not uncommon. Most researchers can tell you a tale (or two) about the time they were in a group for loyal brand-users only to hear first-hand from someone who had never used the product. Since it is unlikely that most of us would undertake the task of managing our own panel, how you work with recruiters and design the screener is ultimately the best way to minimize issues like this.

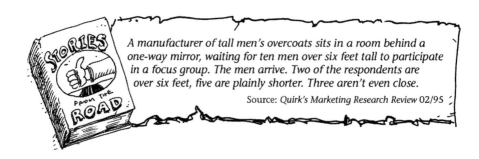

*A manufacturer of tall men's overcoats sits in a room behind a one-way mirror, waiting for ten men over six feet tall to participate in a focus group. The men arrive. Two of the respondents are over six feet, five are plainly shorter. Three aren't even close.*

Source: *Quirk's Marketing Research Review 02/95*

## Are you convinced yet that this is an issue?

Bottom line: If you want to talk to YOUR customers or YOUR prospects, practices like those revealed in this chapter can interfere with your ability to get an authentic voice of the consumer input. What's worse, if you don't ask some tough questions up front, you may never know that you have an impostor sitting in front of you.

Here are some practices that can help improve your recruitment and get you closer to getting the right people in the room:

- Give field agencies plenty of lead time to get the job done. Asking for a fast turn around will increase your chances of running into trouble.

- Be clear about recruiting practices you won't tolerate— including inviting participants' friends and family, using tools like craigslist, and accepting in-bound calls.

- Be sure your screener is complete, clear, and concise. (More on that in the next chapter.)

- Have the field agency record the name of the recruiter and the date of the recruitment.

- Do a double screen and have each recruit verified by a differ-ent person from the first interviewer. Then screen again on the day of the interview. At each step use slightly different questions and a different person if possible.

- Get regular updates and monitor progress so you can fix any issues early while there is still time.

- Ask to randomly monitor recruiting calls. This is sometimes difficult logistically, but it can be useful as a tool for understanding any issues in the screening process.

There is one other strategy to consider, suggested by one of our research experts. Let the facility know that you are going to do the confirmation calls. This step can help ensure that you are satisfied that the right people have been invited to the research. If you find any problems, you still have time to make adjustments, rather than waiting until the day of the group.

Finally, when working with a new recruiter, ask these questions of the recruiters before you decide to use them for your study!

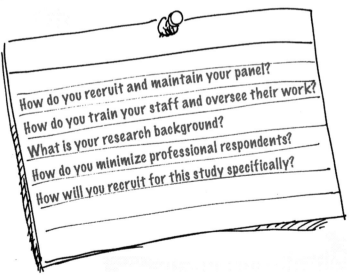

How do you recruit and maintain your panel?
How do you train your staff and oversee their work?
What is your research background?
How do you minimize professional respondents?
How will you recruit for this study specifically?

# CHAPTER 2

# Writing an Air-tight Screener

THE SCREENER is perhaps the most critical document to the success of your project. It clearly identifies the people you want to talk to. This document should be prepared well ahead of time and all key players should be in alignment with its content before you start recruiting. This seems like a simple prescription, but often projects don't work this way.

This chapter will detail some of the most common pitfalls with screeners and what you can do to avoid them to get better recruitment outcomes.

## Do not ask leading questions!

A leading question is one that suggests an answer. For example, "You drink Starbucks, right?" or "You think that recycling is good, right?" In research, the leading question might not be as obvious as these. Instead it might look like this, "Have you eaten at a McDonald's at least once in the past month?" or "Have you participated in research in the past six months?" Questions like these can tip your hand about qualifiers for your study, particularly to panelists who are familiar with the process.

Qualifying questions are a necessary part of any research study because they are the criteria for participation in the group. In a perfect world, we would not worry about how we frame questions, because people would always be honest. But we do not live in a perfect world. Research shows that "professional" responders are becoming more prevalent. Professional respondents are people who do research as a way to make money. They know how the system works and how to "game it" so they can participate in studies and earn the honoraria. Leading questions will increase the risk that you will get professional respondents.

I recently had the opportunity to observe, again, the challenge of getting "honest" recruits. A man recruited for a one-on-one online survey test was quite different from his "recruitment" profile. According to his profile he had a HS degree, earned well into the six-figure range, and took six different pain medications regularly. When we sat down to do the online test, I watched him check every option of every box on almost every screen. Asked why he had done that, he replied that he "liked doing studies as a way to make money . . . and that's how you get in to the study." Sigh.

Even if you believe for some reason that you are immune from "professional" respondents, leading questions still pose a problem. Most people are wired to want to please others so that they might feel accepted and avoid negative judgment. So asking questions where the answer is implied can impact your recruitment. This is especially true when the recruiting is done online and more and more firms are moving to online recruitment. It is quite easy to prevent this from happening. By disguising your questions, you can bury the "correct" answer so it is not as apparent. Here are some ways to do that.

## Use red herrings

If you want to know if someone ate at a specific place, hide that particular place of interest within a list of places. For example,

instead of asking "Did you eat at McDonald's last week?" say, "I am going to read you a list of restaurants you may or may not have eaten at recently. After I read each one, please tell me if you ate at that restaurant in the last week."

Keep the client sponsor blind from the recruiters. Unless the recruiters really need to know the name of the research sponsor, and often they do not, avoid using the sponsor name in any communication or in any documents.

## Stretch the category

Next it is a good idea to stretch the category. If you only list fast food restaurants, you may be tipping your hand that the study is about fast food restaurants. Better to have a mix of options so it is not clear what type of answer or answers you are looking for. This approach also works well for industry questions.

## Industry

**Industry questions** are questions used to exclude people for security reasons—like competitors, the media, really anyone who might have an agenda. The same principle applies here: hide the "correct" response or responses in a list. Let's say the study is for Pepsi and you want to exclude people in the beverage industry. Often, you see a question with the following options: Advertising, Marketing Research, Media, Food and Beverage. This makes it fairly obvious the study is about food and beverage. However, if you were to throw in some other options, like Restaurant, Entertainment, Retail, the study topic becomes less clear.

One other note, if you are concerned about research security or confidentiality (e.g., if you are testing a new product or advertising campaign), it is a good practice to also ask about the occupation of other people close to the respondent such as adults in the household, family members, and friends.

## Use open-ended questions

Consider using open-ended questions rather than providing a list to chose from. This may mean more work on the back end

since open-ended questions are not easily summarized, but it can be worth it in the grand scheme of things.

Back to the McDonald's question. Instead of a closed-ended question, consider asking an open question like, "At what restaurants, if any, have you eaten in the past seven days?" Let them tell you. This is a great way to keep the "correct" response a mystery. If you are recruiting by phone, providing a well-ordered list of options for the interviewer can make things a bit easier. A list that interviewers can mark will save them the time it would take to write down answers. It will also save time coding and tallying them later. *But,* be sure to tell the interviewer that the list should not be read aloud. As an example, your screener question would look like this:

Q. "At what restaurants, if any, have you eaten in the past seven days?"
[Interviewer do not read list]
a.     Burger King
b.     Chili's
c.     McDonald's
d.     Outback Steakhouse
e.     Subway
f.     Other (record verbatim)
g.     Did not eat at a restaurant in the past seven days
NOTE ON QUALIFICATION: Must say c. McDonald's to qualify.

The pre-coded list requires complete trust in the interviewer to accurately classify what the respondent says.

The Bottom Line: The more you lead respondents, the more likely it is that they will take the bait. Tell them what you want to hear and the more likely they are to answer the way they think you want them to. Asking questions in a blind fashion minimizes the chance that you will get a misleading answer, simply because the respondent doesn't know what the "right" answer is.

## Never give away the study goals prematurely

Like the craigslist examples earlier, telling people what you are looking for creates temptation where you don't want it.

Telling people too much about the study is another way you tip your hand about what you are looking for. If someone really wants to participate (either to earn the money or to get a sneak peek), you need to be careful not to provide any clues as to what will qualify a person for the study. Otherwise, expect to have some "professional" respondants lie or misrepresent themselves. Better to keep the subject matter close to the vest for as long as possible. Some recruiters may argue you need to pique the interest of the respondent, but I am not convinced that this is the case. Push back if you hear this. Here are some introductions that are less likely to get you into trouble:

| BEFORE | AFTER |
|---|---|
| We are conducting a study of energy conscious people and want to see if you qualify | We are conducting a study about how people use energy and want to include your input. |
| We are looking for help developing a new product for the insurance industry. | We are recruiting professionals for a group discussion. Can you describe the type of work you do? |
| We are paying married men $100 for their opinions about a television viewing habits. | We are doing a study about home entertainment. I have a few questions first to see if you qualify. |

## Do not reveal qualifiers by terminating the screening interview too early

Let's say you ask for household income. A man answers that he earns less than $50,000 a year. You thank him for his time and hang up. Two things can happen here. First, he could be offended that he doesn't earn enough money for you. Second, he could call his friend (who is also on the panel) and tell her to lie about her income if she wants to get into the study. Friends and family sometimes recruit other people into the panel so they too can earn a few extra dollars.

While it is advisable to put the terminating questions early in the screener in order to avoid wasting time talking to people who ultimately will not qualify, best practice is to ask people a few more questions before you end the screening interview.

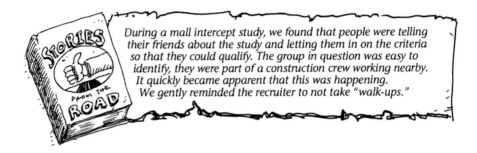

During a mall intercept study, we found that people were telling their friends about the study and letting them in on the criteria so that they could qualify. The group in question was easy to identify, they were part of a construction crew working nearby. It quickly became apparent that this was happening. We gently reminded the recruiter to not take "walk-ups."

This can also happen in centralized facility recruiting. While the exact frequency of this behavior is unknown, it is known to happen. So be careful!

## Avoiding confusing questions

Be clear about what you are asking. The rule of thumb is this: Can you ask five third-graders the same question and have them each interpret it the same way? If not, revise the question.

Here's an example.

| BEFORE | AFTER |
|---|---|
| How often do you buy lottery tickets for yourself or as a gift for someone else? Would you say frequently, sometimes, rarely or never? | How often did you buy lottery tickets for yourself or as a gift for someone else? Would you say once a day or more often, a few times a week, once a week, a few times a month, once a month, less than once a month or never. |

This works better because what may be "sometimes" for one person may not be "sometimes" for another.

Be sure your response options are mutually exclusive and completely exhaustive (MECE). Note that in the "Before" example below, there is no option listed under age 25, and two of the age categories overlap. This is a problem for two reasons, first if you are 24 what do you do? Second if you are 45 what category do you check? If you format your answers to be sure they are MECE, you will avoid these problems.

BEFORE

Which of the following categories includes your age?
25 to 45
45 to 65
65 or older

AFTER

Which of the following categories includes your age?
Under 25
25 to 44
45 to 64
65 or older

## Avoid asking "double barreled" questions

Another question that gets people into trouble is the double-barreled question. These are two questions (or more) in one. For example, "Do you think Candidate X is an honest person and would make a good mayor?" This is two separate questions. First is Candidate X honest? And second would Candidate X made a good mayor? While you may presume that honesty is a condition of being a good mayor, you should not assume everyone else does. Rather, it is possible someone would say Candidate X is honest, but would *not* be a good mayor. These types of questions are easy to fix, although sometimes hard to spot.

To find double-barreled questions, ask yourself if there is more than one possible answer to the same question, like yes to the first part and no to the second part. Next, once you have identified the problem questions, simply split them into smaller, exclusive questions.

This logic also follows for the question responses. Each response should also be singular. For example:

Thinking about your new car, which of the following are you most satisfied with?

    a. the ride and handling,

    b. the safety and security system, or

    c. the design and styling.

The simple fix is to make these three categories into six and allow people to select exactly what they want.

## Here's the key

Nothing will do more to derail your research than bad recruiting. You can have the best guide, the best plan, and the best equipment, but if you are talking to the wrong people you are wasting your time (and everyone else's for that matter).

Take time upfront to make sure that you are clearly communicating your needs to your recruiter and that you have a screener that matches these needs.

# CHAPTER 3

# Working with the Facility and the Field Agency

IN THE 2010 Appleseed Survey of Researchers, nine in ten researchers say they outsource recruiting, making it the most frequently outsourced element of qualitative research. There is good reason for this.

First, facilities maintain respondent databases so they have a pool of willing and able people to call. Basic background information on these people also helps facilities filter their lists to find the best people to invite. In addition, because these prospective respondents have opted in to the panel, they are more likely to cooperate. Unless you are maintaining your own panel, and very few companies do, you will generally find it easier to look outside for this type of support.

Second, field agencies have the staff and the resources to work through the recruiting process for you. It might include an online survey to screen hundreds of people followed by dozens of telephone calls to fill the schedule, not to mention confirmation calls, follow-ups, homework assignments, and even product placements.

Last but not least, facilities have the experience and resources to address any issues that may come up like cancellations and no shows.

So it is best to learn a few tips and tricks for working with the field service to ensure a positive outcome for your own study.

## Online qualitative

**Note** that the process for recruitment for online qualitative and in-person qualitative is similar in theory but different in practice. Both start with a well-written screener and clear recruitment criteria and both types of studies should be recruited with the same rigor.

In-person work typically includes a monetary incentive; online work often includes point-based or sweepstakes incentives. In-person work should include a written confirmation of the day, time, and location of the interview, along with detailed directions (if the respondent needs to travel) and a contact name and number for questions. In-person work also should include a follow-up telephone call to remind participants of their appointment.

Online work would generally only include a confirmation email with a link to the online "location" and a reminder of the date and time. For in-person studies you will generally get a recruitment grid that describes each of the study participants. Larger sample studies (like online qualitative methods such as bulletin boards) may or may not include the same level of per person detail.

The first step in working with a facility is to be sure that you have clearly outlined the study requirements. If you have a solid screener this is a good first step! Now be sure you have discussed and agreed on the actual recruitment process. This will reduce hassles later.

Deliver the screener and review it with the field manager. This review step is frequently skipped because people feel crushed for time or even awkward asking for such a meeting. Spending time reviewing the screener with the field manager always yields better results. For complex screeners, it is best to be involved in or help lead the recruiter training. Also, you might learn something from the locals by taking time to talk through the screener. Collaboration is key; you are all on the same team!

**Don't overload the screener** with too many questions. Research conducted by Fieldwork Inc. suggests that 10 minutes is the optimal length of time for a screener, any longer and people start losing focus. Be sure you edit your questions so that you have a good flow and are not asking unnecessary questions.

**Answer any questions** the field team has like pronunciation, expectations for articulation, skip patterns, and so on. What might be clear to you may not be clear to someone else. Do not assume that everyone knows the correct way to pronounce acetaminophen, Barack Obama or Oconomowac.

**Clearly communicate criteria** for the study, such as no friends and family, no referrals, no cold calls, no ads, and so forth. Don't assume that such rules are standard; they are not. What might be acceptable for you might be unacceptable for someone else and vice versa.

**Avoid asking for a "mix" of respondents.** This is vague. If you want your group of eight to have equal numbers of men and women, say so. If you want at least two men, say so. If you want no more than two retired people, say so. Providing detail can help you get the "mix" you want.

Determine how often you want **updates** (daily, weekly, something in between?) and in what format. During the recruiting period, decide whether you want to see the actual screeners, the recruitment grid, or both. The recruitment grid is a summary of the respondents; the screener is the full screener questionnaire filled out for each respondent. I generally request both: the grids as we go along and the screeners a day prior to the groups.

If you have homework or product placement, be careful that you have given everyone **enough time** for the task—even the people recruited last. Having extra time in the schedule allows you some room to deal with any last minute cancellations and also helps keep the "scrambling" down in filling the seats.

Here is the most important piece of advice for working with recruiters: *Give them enough time to do the job.* Most professional researchers want to deliver a high-quality group. Good recruiters want to be sure you have exactly the right people at your interviews. This takes time. When you crunch the schedule, the pressure on the recruiter increases and you may be compromising quality.

## Grid

**A quick word** on recruitment grids. Over the years, I have seen recruitment grids grow to wallpaper size. This means they can be hard to read, impossible to print, and more prone to error.

Here's a hint: On your screening questionnaire add the following line to the questions that you want included on the summary grid: "Tally and report on recruitment grid." You can also provide a sample grid for the facility to complete. That way you can be sure it is formatted to your liking. On the grid, be sure that you ask for responses and not just numbers. When you want to quickly glance and see who is coming, it can be frustrating to see a column of numbers that you have to look up somewhere else to interpret. Here are some examples:

Do this:

|         | Age         | Education  |
|---------|-------------|------------|
| Lee R.  | under 30    | HS or less |
| Joe P.  | 50 or older | HS or less |
| Matt M. | 30 to 50    | college    |

Not this:

| Age | Education |
|-----|-----------|
| 1   | 6         |
| 8   | 6         |
| 4   | 2         |

And not this either:

| under 30 | 30 to 50 | 50 or older | HS or less | college | grad school |
|:---:|:---:|:---:|:---:|:---:|:---:|
| x | | | x | | |
| | x | | x | | |
| | x | | | | x |

- Be sure your grid has the following information to start: recruiter's name, date of recruitment, and date of confirmation. This way, if you have questions you can easily follow up. It also helps keep track of any "last minute" adds to the list.

- Require recruiting to be complete 3 days before the research session (or some number you feel comfortable with).

- Ask for minimal personal information.

- Always have the date, time, and location on each grid. Multi-city work can easily get confusing if these details are left off.

- Try to keep the grid to one page; otherwise printing becomes a puzzle.

- Ask the facility to use the one column per question format, rather than one column per answer.

| Name | F/M | Age | Educa-tion | HH income | Marital status | Employ-ment | Where grocery shops | Most often for non-food grocery shopping | Products purchased in the past month | Store vs. national (%) |
|---|---|---|---|---|---|---|---|---|---|---|
| Ann T. | F | 40-45 | some college | 70-80K | married | not | Walmart, Stop and Shop | Walmart | aluminum foil, detergent, dog food | store-80% national-50% |
| Pat H. | F | 25-29 | college grad | 40-50K | single | fulltime, renewable energy specialist | Walmart, Costco, Sam's Club | Walmart | plastic wrap, deter-gent, rug cleaner | store-10% national-0% |
| Tina B. | F | 45-49 | high school | 80K+ | married | fulltime, social worker | Walmart, Target, Kmart, Family Dollar | Walmart | aluminum foil, plastic wrap, cat food | store-80% national-50% |

- Be sure the date is updated on each so you know what version you are looking at.

- Ask for a summary of key groups. For example, if you want to have an even number of men and women, the facility should show the count for easy reference.

---

Time, cost, and quality are always at odds. It is hard, if not impossible to optimize all three of these. Therefore, you have to think about where you want to compromise. If you pressure the facility, the recruiters may feel the need to relax their quality control measures to deliver a room full of bodies. By building in more time to the recruitment process you limit the stress many of these field services are under to fill seats. Systems with checks and balances in place perform better than those without. Having multiple people touch the same respondent makes it harder for liars and cheaters to be seated in your interview. People are less likely to cut corners if they know someone is reviewing their work.

# CHAPTER 4

# Incentives:
# What to Pay and Why

NOW that you know how to find the right people for your project, you need to determine what to pay them. Two things motivate people who agree to participate in research studies. One, they want to tell you what they think; two, they want to get paid. I bet that you can guess which of these is the most motivating factor.

Unlike online studies which reward people by giving them "points," in-person qualitative rewards people by paying them for their time. Most people will not accept a study invitation unless they know they are going to be compensated for their time and participation.

In a study reported in *Quirk's Marketing Research Review* in May 1990, two-thirds of people said they accepted the study invitation because of the gratuity. I believe these numbers are even higher today because of increased economic pressures and higher levels of familiarity with focus groups in general.

When you set up your recruitment, you may be asked for the "incidence" rate. This is the likelihood of finding the people who meet your specifications. A low incidence means that those people are harder to find (fewer of them in the population). A higher incidence means that those people are easier to find (more of them in the population). Finding a man who regularly buys beer is easier than finding a man who regularly buys wine coolers.

As a rule of thumb, populations with lower incidence are more expensive to recruit than populations with higher incidence. Some panels have been developed with this in mind. These specialty panels help you target your recruiting efforts better and are more efficient with your dollars. If you are looking for a specific group such as lawyers, Hispanics, or medical specialists, consider using a specialty panel. Check *www.greenbook.org* for a list of suppliers by specialty.

Incidence is one thing, but how do you determine how much someone's time is worth? Put yourself in their shoes. Let's say that you want to interview mothers who have been to a theme park at least once in the past year, have a household income of at least $100,000 annually, have children under age 5, and live within 30 miles of the facility. Let's also say that you want to interview each in her home at noon on a Wednesday, for two hours. Is this worth $150, $300, or $500?

## How do you decide?

The first place to start is with the facility. Most of the time the recruiters or field managers will have the best sense of what is required to get the people you are targeting to participate. Start by asking what they recommend and how they arrived at that figure. If their suggestion is outside your budget, try to understand what type of wiggle room you have. But don't cheap out here. You will regret it when research day comes. The adage, "you get what you pay for" applies to research too.

Think about the monetary value your participant places on her time. You will have a hard time getting professionals who earn $200 an hour to take time off from work to talk with you for $50 an hour. This is true not just of lawyers and accountants but trades people too—plumbers, electricians, landscapers, and small business owners. Check out *www.salary.com* for a listing of typical salaries to get a better idea of what you are up against. But the bottom line is this: Show your respect for people and their time by paying a fair honorarium.

Note that some professions, like physicians, might be discouraged from taking cash payment for their time. Instead, they might opt for a charitable donation in their name. Your recruiter can work with you on these logistics.

Even non-working people incur costs when participating in research. Imagine asking a stay-at-home mom to come to a central location to do an interview. What does it cost her? Does she need to hire a babysitter? Does she need to pay for parking? Does she need to take a taxi? A train? How far will she need to drive to get to the location? What if you want to visit her at home? Is she preparing the house for your arrival? Is she spending time cleaning for your arrival? Is she hiring a sitter to watch the baby during the interview? All of these factors come into play.

Listen to what one panelist said when asked about the incentives and how they impact her participation.

> I enjoy these groups, but babysitters cost money and I couldn't really justify $15 to $25 in babysitting, transportation, and time away from my family if there was no pay.

Source: *Quirk's Marketing Research Review*, May 1990

## Other considerations: Homework or prep work

If you are going to ask your respondents to do any type of work ahead of time, they should get extra compensation. Not compensating for homework decreases cooperation and increases the likelihood that people will skip the assignment. Be clear in the screener what the incentive is for the respondent, both for the interview and for the pre-work you are assigning. Here is one way to phrase the honoraria: "You will be paid $75 for your participation in the interview and $25 for doing the homework assignment."

### Prizes!

Another effective compensation strategy when assigning homework is to tell respondents that the person with the "best" homework will get a prize. This approach can help motivate people to give more thought to and spend more time on the homework. After all, there's a prize! Here's some language you can use. "You will be paid $75 for your participation in the interview. In addition, the moderator will give out a $50 gift card to the person with the best homework assignment."

Note that honoraria are generally paid to respondents at the time of the session, so you should also be prepared to provide this money to the recruiter or the facility well before the interviews take place.

As a last word here, if the study sponsor is comfortable being named at the end of the interview, you can build a great deal of good will by giving participants a small gift from the sponsor company. Food samples, free products, branded pens or bags, t-shirts, discounts, or free coupons always go over well. Just about anything is appreciated and really delights participants.

## Ideas for incentives

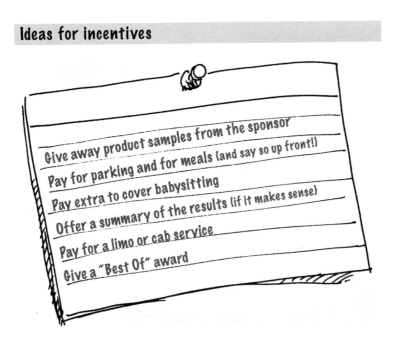

Give away product samples from the sponsor

Pay for parking and for meals (and say so up front!)

Pay extra to cover babysitting

Offer a summary of the results (if it makes sense)

Pay for a limo or cab service

Give a "Best Of" award

# CHAPTER 5

# Scheduling: The Where, the When, and the Why

IF YOU are doing work that requires someone to be present on a specific date and at a certain time, scheduling is a challenge you have to deal with. People are busier than ever, working longer hours and "connected" constantly. Add to that kids with soccer practice, piano lessons, homework, and an SAT tutor and you start to see where your research interview fits in to the grand scheme of things.

All of these factors have added to the appeal of asynchronous online qualitative, but we'll cover that topic in Chapter 17. For now, let's consider scheduling as it relates to in-person work and how to optimize it!

## Time and money

To get people to agree to participate in your study, paying them for their time is number one; scheduling is a close number two. For some people, it may be the deal breaker.

*Enjoyed the session a lot . . . the gratuity is helpful, but working this into my schedule is the bigger issue on participating.*

Source: *Quirk's Marketing Research Review,* May 1990

## Tips for scheduling central location work

When you schedule your study, your facility or recruiter may be able to help you think through some of the logistics. But in general, think about what time makes sense from your respondents' perspective. Professionals will need to talk to you before or after work. Moms will have more free time during the school day when their kids are away.

Besides your own respondents, think about the team that might be observing. What works for them? What travel is required? If you set up the interviews to start at 11 a.m., do you need to travel the day before? Are you planning to do a debrief at the end of the day? If so, you probably want to be done early enough that people are not dozing during the debriefing.

Show respondents that you are sensitive to their time constraints. In the confirmation letter be sure you include clear, accurate directions and approximate travel times. This helps participants plan ahead so that they can arrive on time. Note any streets that may be congested due to construction or traffic. Be sure that your directions include details like where to park and where to go when they arrive. Have the street address for GPS mapping and provide a contact name and number so people can let you know if they are lost or running late.

Provide more substantial food during mealtimes and let people know ahead of time that food will be available. This helps people fit research interviews into their schedules more easily. Even if you are not holding your session over mealtime, always offer drinks and snacks. It is hospitable and shows that you want to make the experience pleasant.

Tell respondents to plan to arrive 10 to 15 minutes before the start of the interview. This builds in a cushion for late arrivals. Try to schedule enough time between groups in case you need to run long after a late start. If you think the session is going to take 45 minutes, schedule an hour. Better to let people go early than to hold them over, or risk people needing to leave before you are finished.

Be sure that the waiting area is comfortable and has reading material. This makes the time pass faster and your participants will be more refreshed and relaxed when the interview starts. If space allows, consider having groups sit together at a table in the waiting area to get to know each other ahead of time. This early rapport can help relax respondents and get them ready to be open in the group.

## Break the ice

**Speaking of rapport,** when planning the group, be sure you build in time in the beginning to break the ice. Diving right in to the topic without having established trust and rapport with the respondents will make the interview more challenging.

Two more important scheduling considerations have to do not with the respondents but with the observer/client. If you have people coming to watch the interviews, tell them to arrive early.

Ideally you want everyone seated in the back room before respondents arrive. The last thing you want a room full of respondents to see is someone walking in with a backpack embossed with the client's name. Second, when planning your research events for the day, decide if you need to build in time to debrief. This can be done either between interviews or at the end of the day. This part of the day should be planned ahead of time so you can be sure that you have booked the facility space for the proper amount of time.

One last thing to consider when scheduling your research is contingencies for no shows or last-minute cancellations. We all know that when we plan a party, not everyone who RSVPs will actually be there. It is the same in research. Over recruiting can help you be sure to have a full set of respondents on the day of the research. It is also insurance in case you do a re-screen and find you need to send someone home. For focus groups, research speak is to say "recruit 10 to seat 8" or "recruit 8 to seat 6." This language means that the facility will recruit 10 people and you will take 8 in to the research. If all 10 people show up on time, you will need to pay everyone. But this is a minor expense compared with not having the right number of people.

The approach if you are doing one-on-one interviews is slightly different. Individual interviews are usually shorter than focus groups, so common practice is to recruit someone to be available over several interviews in case of a cancellation or no-show. These people are called floaters.

## Special considerations for individual interviews

Here's a typical one-on-one floater scenario. You have three interviews scheduled between the hours of 4 p.m. and 7 p.m. One starts at 4 p.m., the next starts at 5 p.m. and the third starts at 6 p.m. If any one of these cancel, you have an empty slot. If you have a floater—someone paid to be on hand at the facility from 4 to 7—you could fill the missing slot with the floater. Floaters should meet all the qualifications for participation and should be paid more than a regular participant because they are giving up more of their time. Typically fees for the floaters are about two or three times that of a regular respondent. So if you are doing 45-minute one-on-one interviews for $75, you would pay your floater $150 to $200 to be on hand for the two plus hours. Be sure that you explain ahead of time that the floater may or may not be called to do the interview.

## Tips for scheduling on site work (in home for example)

Over the course of your work, it is likely that not all of your research interviews will be at a central location. In the 2010 Appleseed survey, respondents told us that while close to 60 percent of their qualitative work was done in a central location, more than a quarter was done in the respondent's home, in stores or other locations. The rest was done online or by telephone. Scheduling any type of off-site interview poses new challenges along with those discussed above.

First, be realistic about how many different locations you get to each day. Too often I have seen clients try to jam in interviews so as to minimize travel expenses and too often I have seen clients stressed out trying to get from Point A to Point B on time. I too have fallen victim.

Driving a rental car on assignment in the Tampa Bay area, I followed its GPS system's directions only to find myself headed towards a very long bridge, with no chance of escape. This navigation error made us late for our next appointment. More importantly, it made us look inconsiderate to our respondent.

GPS has limitations, especially in dense urban areas, if the weather is overcast or raining, or when it just plain stops working. Get good directions the old-fashioned way, too, and keep a map on hand when travelling to unfamiliar areas. And stay in touch with your appointments if you're delayed.

To minimize hassles, it is best to work with a recruiter who understands the local geography. That way you can get some help as you plan your day. You should request that interviews are scheduled based on proximity as much as possible. Also, ask the recruiter to provide detailed driving directions as well as two phone numbers for the people you are visiting.

On the day you are scheduled to do the interview, you should always call ahead to introduce yourself and the team. Confirm that you are on your way and ask for any landmarks or instructions that will help you in your navigation. Always let your respondent know if there are any delays. This is not only good manners but also goes a long way to putting the respondent at ease. Having heard from you ahead of time makes the first meeting more pleasant.

## If you are doing shop-alongs

**A shop-along** is a type of observational research where you go with someone to buy a product. This can be useful when you want to understand what happens at the point of sale.

Be sure you have scheduled adequate time to travel to and from the store, find parking, and for the shopping exercise itself. Like any other interview, plan for more time than you think you will need. Better to leave early than stay late.

Unlike central location interviews, you should avoid doing home interviews during mealtime, bed time, get to school/work time. Think about how hectic someone's life may be and be sensitive in scheduling.

Be sure you also consider the other occupants and distractions in the home. If you are interviewing a mom, do you want the kids there or not? If you are talking to a man about life insurance, do you want his spouse to be available for questions? If you are doing a study about frozen pizza do you want to talk to the teenagers in the house as well as the primary grocery shopper? This is important not just from a research content point of view, but also for quality. You may find that you gain valuable insight by hearing from multiple people in the household.

However, other people may distract your primary subject. That could interrupt the flow and quality of your interview. In addition, you might have a hard time using the event recording if you pick up outside noise like a baby crying or kids playing Xbox.

## Tips for scheduling executive interviews

If you are doing in-person executive or business interviews you must do your best to be flexible, professional, and cordial (as you should be for all interviews). Schedule changes are not uncommon, particularly for physicians and senior executives. The more you roll with the punches, the more likely you are to get the interview. Often you will not even speak to your research subjects until you meet them. Rather you will work through assistants. Be sure they have all the information they need to manage the appointment. Always call ahead to confirm the date and time and be careful not to over pack the day. That will leave you more flexible and able to make adjustments if schedules change.

## Scheduling work by telephone

Interviews by phone are another fairly common way to do individual interviews. These are used most often for low-incidence populations, when you need a diverse geographic mix but cannot travel, for groups that are hard to schedule, or when budgets are tight. Use the same scheduling criteria you would for in-person work with careful attention to communicating how the phone call will run and any special instructions. Specifically, are you going to call the respondents? Will they call you? Will they call a conference line? Conference lines are useful because of the many features they support, not the least of which is audio recording capabilities. They also allow for multiple people to join either as participants or silent listeners. Just be sure you disclose all people on the line! In addition, they are often toll-free which is a benefit for the respondent.

Even if you plan to use a conference line, be sure you have two contact numbers for the respondent in case there are any changes or you need to reach them. It is not uncommon for someone to be sitting waiting for your call, rather than dialing into the line. Having a contact number is critical to getting your schedule back on track.

You should also be clear about what you expect from respondents during the call. If they need to have access to a computer or the Internet, tell them. If you need them to take notes tell them. If you prefer they talk to you on a landline, and not a cell phone, tell them. Setting expectations up front makes the process better all around and eliminates any frustration.

## Scheduling work online

One of the benefits of online work is that you remove many of the obstacles of in-person work—namely traveling and scheduling. Online work is typically done asynchronously; that is, people participate at their convenience within certain parameters. (The exception are online focus groups which happen in real time.

More on that later!) They can answer questions or reply to what other people say on their own schedule, rather than on a specific day at a specific time.

If you are doing online work, like a bulletin board or chat room, consider your respondents when determining the schedule and the requirements. People who work may have limited availability, either because of firewalls at the office or because of the type of work they do. Someone who is on the road most of the day may not be able to be online as often as someone with a desk job. Other people may have *more* time at work than they do at home because of responsibilities they need to tend to in the house. School-aged respondents probably are less likely to be available between 8 a.m. and 3 p.m. and it might be unrealistic to ask them to check in more than twice a day. You also want to consider what days of the week are most appropriate. If the board is going to be open for several days, is the weekend better or during the week?

Bottom line: Keep the respondent in mind and communicate expectations clearly up front.

## Tips for scheduling research

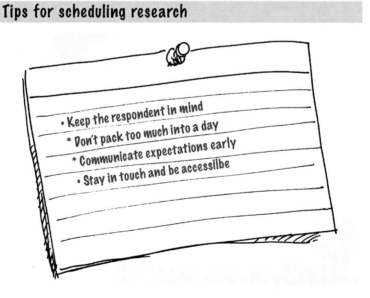

- Keep the respondent in mind
- Don't pack too much into a day
- Communicate expectations early
- Stay in touch and be accessilbe

# CHAPTER 6

# Confidentiality: A Two-Way Street

CASRO, the Council of American Survey Research Organizations, lists two things under the heading, "responsibilities to clients." The first is confidentiality and the second is privacy. These are tenets of marketing research and must be upheld, even if your organization is not a part of CASRO and even if you are not a market research supplier.

At the foundation of privacy is the understanding that an individual's personal information is never shared outside of the confines of the research project. This allows respondents the anonymity to speak freely and comfortably. Here is a basic list of what you can do and what you can't do:

## What you **CAN** do

Video and audiotape with prior permission.

Refer to respondents by first name.

Ask for and record non-identifying information.

Use material for research-purposes only (as specified in the agreement the respondent signs).

## What you CANNOT do

Refer to respondent by first and last name.

Share respondent information (like address or email).

Use respondent contact information for any reason outside the project.

Sell or share respondent lists or information to another third party.

Use a person's likeness for advertising or sales purposes, without consent.

If you are using a central location, the facility hostess will have a form for participants to sign before they participate in your research. This form details the nature of the agreement between the researcher and the participant. Review this form before you begin your work to be sure it covers all you need it to cover. If you find it does not, you should develop your own material and ask the facility to have respondents sign your form. Lawyers can be helpful here. The fee is worth it because these documents will serve you in the long run.

Whether you develop your own release form or use the form that the facility has, be sure that your release reveals (at a minimum) the following three disclosures: video and audio taping will be used; participants will be paid for their opinions; and, any information shared or discussed is completely confidential.

In addition to getting written consent before the interview starts, be sure you begin each session with a recap of the ground rules. Remind people that there are microphones and video cameras recording what happens in the room and that there are people watching and listening either behind the one-way mirror or remotely. Tell the participants that all information is for research only and that video materials are shared only with the research team. Confirm for them that information collected (including video and audio) will not be used outside the research itself without prior consent. No uploading funny clips to YouTube, though the temptation might arise!

### Releases

If you want to use any material at a later date in promotional material or advertising (or think you might), a different release is needed. But beware; going this route can impact your cooperation rate. Remember these are research volunteers, not actors.

Confidentiality is a two-way street. Just as you are telling respondents that you respect their information it is important that you tell them that this is your expectation of them as well. Remind your interviewees that they are being paid for their opinions and that the discussion is completely confidential, including what they might see or hear from you or from each other. Consider limiting the use of cell phones, cell phone cameras, and require respondents to agree to these provisions up front.

If respondents are uncomfortable agreeing to the terms or do not want to sign the release form, they are free to withdraw from the research session. Research is voluntary and respondents cannot be forced to participate. You are better off moving on rather than including a respondent who will not agree to the terms of the project.

One last word: Often you might be doing research over several days at the same facility. While it may be easiest to leave your materials there, do not assume that they will be secured. Be sure you take any necessary precaution with sensitive materials. Leaving things behind with the assumption they are secure could land you in a heap of trouble.

## Computer safety

If you are working on a public computer (like those at the facility or even the hotel) you want to be very careful that you are not leaving a trail of cookie crumbs.

While I am not an expert in computer security, I advise you to do the following:

1. avoid using public computers or unsecured wifi networks whenever possible;

2. empty the cache or clear the history from the web browser; and

3. if you are on a public computer and need to work on a document, rather than simply deleting it, save a file with the same name but with no contents. That will overwrite your material on the hard drive and make it harder for someone to uncover your work at a later time. Be sure you are doing this in the right spot. It would be a shame to lose the information you have on your jump drive.

Try this next time you need to use a public computer. After you are done, re-open the software (whether it is Word, Excel, or Adobe). Go to "recent files" and see if your document is there. If it is and if you can open it from the hard drive, you have left a trail that someone can follow.

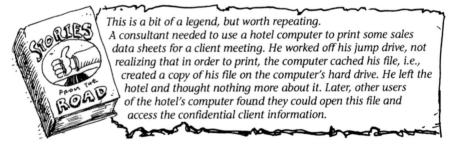

*This is a bit of a legend, but worth repeating.*
*A consultant needed to use a hotel computer to print some sales data sheets for a client meeting. He worked off his jump drive, not realizing that in order to print, the computer cached his file, i.e., created a copy of his file on the computer's hard drive. He left the hotel and thought nothing more about it. Later, other users of the hotel's computer found they could open this file and access the confidential client information.*

# CHAPTER 7

# Respondent Management and Communication

ONCE you have laid the groundwork for the recruitment and set the schedule, you can sit back and let the facility do its work—sort of. The recruiter's job is to get the respondents that you outlined in your screener on the date and time you need them. Using all the resources at their disposal and depending on your needs, this process will take one to two weeks. Any longer than that and you will find people forgot or scheduled something else. Any sooner and you are rushing. This valley between the recruitment and the interview is the focus of this chapter.

What now? Well put yourself in the shoes of the respondents. What would you like to see happen next? Here are a few thoughts.

## Before the research

Send a confirmation email or letter. Real letters, delivered by real people are preferred, if you have time. They are more professional and personal than an email.

Your confirmation letter should be personalized to the respondent (as in "Dear Mrs. Anderson" rather than "Dear Respondent"). Your letter should include all the relevant details about the session and what is expected. It should also include the name and number of a person they can contact with questions.

If you are doing in-home interviews the confirmation is just as critical, but might include slightly different details. Below are examples of what to include in each type of confirmation letter.

---

**CONFIRMATION FOR IN-HOME INTERVIEW**

▷    Date and Start and End Times

▷    Who is Arriving

▷    What to Expect (home tour, activities, filming)

▷    Who Should be Home (kids, spouse, friends)

▷    Reminder of Incentive

▷    Contact Name and Phone Number

---

**CONFIRMATION FOR CENTRAL LOCATION INTERVIEW**

▷    Date and Start and End Times

▷    Location and Directions

▷    Parking Information and Fees

▷    Onsite Navigation (Where to go once you arrive)

▷    What to Bring (glasses, products, homework)

▷    Reminder of Incentive

▷    Contact Name and Phone Number

---

In some cases you may be preparing this material; in others, the facility or the recruiter will do it for you. Either way, you should be sure of three things: first that a confirmation is sent in writing, second that it sets the right tone, and third it provides the respondent with useful information. Don't be shy about asking to review the material before it goes out. Even if you feel like you are being a micro-manager, at the end of the day, taking extra care here will help your outcome, especially if you have not worked with the facility or the recruiter before.

Finally, a telephone confirmation call is critical. A telephone call is most commonly used to confirm attendance and answer any last minute questions that the respondent might have. This may be your only confirmation in cases when there is no time to do an email or mail confirmation. Calls should be made as close to the research as possible to be sure that there are no changes.

*I used to conduct large scale in-person evaluations of marketing material. We would typically invite 50 or more high school juniors to participate. To accommodate this group size, we often did the research in hotels. Now, imagine you are the parent of one of these students recruited to look at college materials at a local Holiday Inn for two hours, and then be paid $100. Sounds weird, right?*

*Well, this is where a professional confirmation can really help validate your work. Today, COPPA regulations are in place which changed the rules, but you get the idea. What might seem innocent to you, might look suspicious to someone else.*

## The day of the research

If you are doing a session in someone's home, the interview team leader (usually the moderator) should place a brief call when the team is on the way. This can help put the respondent at ease that you have "met" by phone. Think blind date. Better to have some contact than none. This pre-arrival call also tells the respondent when to expect you and gives you a chance to clarify driving directions if needed.

Research at a facility is different. It is *not* standard practice for the researcher to make the confirmation calls. Rather the facility staff will do this step. They are the hosts in this case. They are better equipped to answer any questions that need answering, like directions or scheduling. If you decide you want to have contact with the respondents before the interview, discuss this up front with the recruiters. You want to be sure that respondents aren't bombarded by calls and that they have a clear understanding of who to talk to if issues arise. Too many cooks will spoil the soup!

## Research etiquette

Send confirmation in writing to all study participants

Be sure the letter has all the details

Place a call the day of or night before to confirm

Provide a contact name and number to call if needed

# CHAPTER 8

# Working with the Facility Hostess

AS YOU can tell by now, the facility staff holds a lot of cards. They are the link between you and your respondents. They make the first impression. They set the tone early on. However, I have yet to see recruiters or a facility manager presenting research results. The buck ultimately will still stop with you as the researcher or project leader.

Here are some ideas for managing the relationship with the hostess to achieve optimal results.

## The Four Bees

**Be nice.** Enough said.

**Be clear.** Even if you think you are being clear, be clearer. Be sure that you make requests in writing and review all the material with the project manager. This can prevent misunderstandings moving forward.

**Be in touch.** Once the process has started, you need to stay in touch with the recruiter. Explain up front the frequency with which you want updates. I usually ask for daily reports. This way you can see if there are any issues and head them off at the pass, before it is too late.

**Be reasonable.** Everyone wants to do his or her best to make the research successful. Even the best-laid plans might not go smoothly, so be reasonable about what can and cannot be done.

## Finding the right facility

Besides being pleasant, accessible, and clear, there are some other things you can do to optimize your work with the facility and the facility hostess. Before you engage a facility or recruiter, check them out. There are a few ways to do that.

Impulse Research Corporation of California maintains ratings for over 800 facilities in the U.S. and abroad and annually publishes the scores based on input from thousands of moderators. Ratings include six items: recruiting, personnel, physical space, location, food service, and value. In addition, Impulse calculates an overall score. The Impulse Survey also offers lists of recruiters and videographers. This information can be invaluable when working in a new market. (To add your own feedback or to get a copy of the results go to the website: *www.impulsesurvey.com.*)

Another resource for finding the right facility is the *Green-Book.* This is a comprehensive list of more than 1,500 research firms broken down by category, specialty, and location (to name just a few of the searches available). The New York chapter of the American Marketing Association publishes the *GreenBook.* You can find out more about it (or do a search for a facility) at *www.greenbook.org.* There is also a print edition available for purchase if you want to go that route.

*Quirk's Marketing Research Review (www.quirks.com)* is another excellent source for finding qualitative support—including facilities, moderators, and panels. The search is straightforward and lets you enter criteria like facility location, location features (test kitchen for example), or moderator specialty. Quirk's also has a large library of articles related to qualitative research.

Another resource worth checking into is the Qualitative Research Consultants Association, a.k.a. QRCA. They are a nonprofit groups of qualitative users and moderators that provide information and resources to the qualitative industry. If you are looking for a moderator for a project, this is a great resource. You can search by location, industry specialization, subgroup, or population expertise, and methodology. You can also find people with fluency in a specific language. The QRCA is also open for membership to researchers who specialize in qualitative work. Check it out at *www.qrca.org.*

Besides these resources, ask for referrals from colleagues and friends. Post questions on LinkedIn and other professional networking sites. Visit and read facility websites; better still, go and visit the facility. If you cannot go in person, ask for images of the rooms (front and back rooms). Ask about the background of key staff. Ask about quality control procedures and training. Think about the facility location, specifically accessibility, and the zip codes it draws from (this is often on the facility web site). All things are not equal in the world of research facilities. Keep your eyes open going in and you should be okay!

Check to see what professional memberships the company holds.

If you are working with a group that is not part of a professional research organization, you can hardly expect them to uphold industry tenets.

# SECTION 2

# Getting to the Insight—
# It's in There

# CHAPTER 9

# Guiding the Discussion

THE FOCUS of this book so far has been on the preparation that needs to happen before you endeavor to do qualitative work. Once a solid foundation has been laid, it is time to get to the guts of the project—finding the insight. That is, getting respondents to tell you what you need to hear: the truth. People always have the answer, so long as the researcher is asking the right question. Henry Ford once said, "If I'd asked people what they wanted, they would have said faster horses." He, of course, went on to create the Model T.

Later in this section of the book we will talk about how to help consumers give you answers by asking the right question (or not asking a question at all). But first, let's talk about the building block for any interview—the discussion guide, also known as the moderator guide, or the interview guide.

The first thing to know about the guide is that is it NOT a questionnaire. Questionnaires are generally one-sided. When administering a questionnaire, the interviewer asks a question and the respondent gives an answer. While the question flow might change based on a participant's answers, there is no conversation. This is not bad, it just is. Most questionnaires are for large sample studies where the goal is to get information that can be quantified, analyzed, and summarized numerically.

Discussion guides are a different beast entirely. The goal of a questionnaire is *quantification*, the goal of the discussion guide is *discussion*. The guide should be structured enough to be sure you are meeting your objective and loose enough to allow you to go where the conversation leads.

Imagine you are an actor. On Tuesday and Saturday you are performing Shakespeare. On Monday and Friday you perform with an improv group. Shakespeare requires a specific dialogue and you would follow a tight script. Each night you do the same exact show. But improv would be different each night. While you would have an idea and general plan for what you were going to do, you would feed off the people in the improv group and even in the audience. No two shows would be the same. It is the same in qualitative research. Even with the same guide, no two sessions are ever the same. And that's okay.

## Part of a discussion guide

While discussion guides are as individual as the project itself, certain elements are (almost) always included.

# Ground rules

No matter if you are in a facility or in someone's home, you should always start by explaining the session. Tell people what to expect. Explain how long the session will last. Explain if there are cameras and microphones. Explain that the recording is for research only.

Explain any additional people in the room or behind the one-way mirror (you don't have to be specific but you have to let them know they are there). Be sure that they know you will keep their information confidential and encourage them to speak openly.

Introduce yourself (if you are the moderator) and explain your role, and last but not least, remind everyone there are no right or wrong answers. This is also a good time to ask if anyone is new to the research experience. Some people may have done interviews before and be familiar with the process; others may be new and might have more anxiety. It is good to know this up front.

# Introductions

After you have given everyone the lay of the land, you should start by asking them to introduce themselves to you and to each other. When you do introductions, think about what else you might want to know about that person. This is often a good time for respondents to share something about

their lives especially if it is related to the study topic. If you are talking to moms, you might ask them to tell you about their children. If you are talking to foodies, you might ask for their favorite cuisine. In other instances, you might want to start even more general and ask them for their name and one word a friend would use to describe them; or their favorite spot to relax; or their dream job. These introductions generally don't take all that long, but they are important in breaking the ice and establishing some relevance for the respondents.

## DON'T DO THIS!

To protect the identity of the respondent, be sure that you do not ask for any personally identifiable information like—last name, phone number, address, etc. Not only are such details of no use in the study, they violate the agreement you made to keep their remarks anonymous.

## The conclusion

This is the only other part of the guide that is "standard." In this section you wrap up the interview, thank people for their time and instruct them on where to go to check out (if they are in a central facility).

The rest of the guide will be set up in whatever way matches the study objectives. But most guides follow the "funnel" structure; that is, they start off general and get more specific as they go. There are a few reasons for this:

## Trust

By building the discussion from general to specific you help to build trust between the interviewer and the respondent and among the respondents. Having this foundation of trust will help you uncover more closely held thoughts and feelings as people will be more relaxed and open. The last time you went to a dinner party, you probably met some people you did not know well. Chances are you talked to them first about some generic topics such as the weather, the menu, maybe traffic, and then, after breaking the ice, you probably talked about family, common interests, common friends. Depending on the person, you might have moved on to more sensitive topics like politics or religion. It is human nature to start discussions general and move into more sensitive topics once you feel comfortable. It is the same in an interview setting.

# Bias

Depending on your study goals, it is important to think about bias and the role it plays in the flow of the groups. As an example, imagine you are interested in how consumers react to a new ad that highlights a safety feature on a product. Your study objective is to find out whether that safety feature is relevant and how consumers respond to the ad about that feature.

Approach #1: Show the ad and get feedback.

Approach #2: Ask consumers about the features that matter to them, discuss, then show the ad and get feedback.

In the first approach, you are prompting consumers with an ad highlighting a specific feature (e.g., safety) and asking them to react. They are not primed at all having spent no time talking about what features matter to them.

In the second approach, by starting more generally, you can wait to hear if safety is a feature that matters to people without the aid of a prompt like the ad.

Another common scenario where bias can be present is when you want to talk generally about the category and then drill down to a specific brand or brands. If you start with the brand too soon, you may be tipping your hat to the study sponsor and biasing the discussion.

Again, your study objectives will help you decide the way to go, but be sure you consider bias in the flow of the guide.

## Why you might not want to use the funnel

If you want to get an *immediate* reaction to something (like an advertisement, prototype or a concept), you might not want to spend any time discussing products or the product category. When making the decision about whether to use the funnel or jump right in, think about the study objectives first and let the objectives be your guide.

## Follow-up questions

When you design a guide (or evaluate one) you want to think about the flow of individual questions as well as the flow of the overall guide. Often you will want to hear first what people think on their own, and then go on to ask follow up questions based on their answers. These follow-up questions are often referred to as probes. Here's an example from a study where consumers tested a new storage container for a week before the group. This part of the study asked consumers about their experiences testing the product at home.

## General comparison

Based on your at home "test drive" how would you say this new container compares to what you are using now?

**PROBE:**

Ease of cleaning
Ease of use
Storage
Color
Durability
Quality of material

In this example, the question starts general to get the consumers first thoughts about their product test. But having a list that the moderator can refer to, helps to make sure that any specific features not mentioned are covered. After the initial conversation is over, you might ask people to talk about their experiences washing the container, or what they thought of the color. This way nothing is left out of the discussion.

Another way to use probes when developing a discussion guide is to think about how you want to handle information you may hear. Here's an example:

Let's go around the room. Would you tell [store] to carry this product or not?

**PROBE:**

Let's split the room—the no's on the right and the yes'es on the left. As a team, write down the reasons why you say no or yes to this product. We'll talk about them together after you finish.

[When finished]: No's you go first, why do you say [the store] should not carry this product? Yes's what would you say to convince the no's to change their mind now that you know what their objections are?

This example shows one plan of attack; you may come up with others. The point here is that if you think through these types of scenarios you can be more confident that your objectives will be met at the end of the session.

## Formatting

One last word on the guide. If you are moderating, you will, over time, develop your own style and figure out what does work for you and what does not work for you in terms of formatting your discussion guide.

**A few hints in the meantime:**

Use a large, easy-to-read font so you can read the guide and find your place quickly.

Avoid using the client name anywhere on the guide.

Start each section on a new page so you can follow along easily and not fumble with pages.

# CHAPTER 10

# Homework and Exercises: Not Just for First Graders

HOMEWORK and exercises during the interview can help energize your respondents, get deeper insights, and encourage creativity beyond words. Approaches that take us outside of the limits of language can unlock a treasure trove of insight. This chapter explores how and when to use homework and exercises and some best practices to keep in mind.

## Homework 101

Of the researchers surveyed in the 2010 Appleseed study, 92 percent said they have given some sort of assignment as pre-work in the last year making it the most popular tool or technique!

There are many good reasons to have people do work ahead of the interview. Here are just a few:

- *To give respondents sufficient time to complete a task.* Exercises like those discussed below, often require time. This is a great reason for the work to be completed pre-interview.

- *To get real-life input.* If you want feedback on a product or prototype, you might be better off having people use the product in their everyday life, rather than in the research environment. Sending products out ahead of time for a "test-drive" can help you learn more about how that product really performs and fits into a consumer's life.

- *To allow people more creative freedom in completing the task.* Most homework assignments require specific materials to complete, like magic markers, tape, magazines, photographs, and so on. If you let respondents have free access to materials (rather than what you might provide), you will find you get better results and higher engagement.

- *To heighten their awareness of events or activities that may live under the radar.* In other words, priming them for the interview. Research often attempts to understand motivations behind routine behaviors and low-involvement decisions. Asking people to keep a journal, take pictures, or describe events as they happen can reveal motivations and yield deeper insights that you may not get otherwise, especially after the fact.

- *To reduce any undue influence from others within the group.* Doing exercises in a group setting (or even in a one-on-one setting with a moderator) might stifle some participants. Having people work in the comfort of their homes without fear of judgment can make the process more open and creative and ultimately, more honest.

- *To help groups bond.* I have found that people often talk about their projects with each other in the waiting room and build rapport they may not have otherwise. This can kick start your group—sort of an early icebreaker.

- *To help select individuals for the final set of interviews.* Another use for pre-work is to determine the best candidates for the full study. For example, if you are doing ethnography you may want to re-screen respondents first. By giving home-work or pre-work you can preview the consumer ahead of time and get a sense of what is to come. Think of it as "casting" participants. And if you are groaning to yourself thinking, "this is research, we don't cast for research," we can agree to disagree. Casting in this way can help you avoid an interview with the wrong person. If you decide to use pre-work as a re-screen, be upfront with the respondent ahead of time. Always pay people for their time and effort even if they are not selected for the final round. This technique is well suited to one of the many online qualitative tools avail-able. See Chapter 18 for more about online qualitative.

## DON'T DO THIS!

If your reason for assigning pre-work is that you have too much to cover during the main inter-view, caution! Even though the respondents are doing work at home, the value of the exercise lies primarily in the dialogue between you and them. Be sure you have enough time to listen to why they did what they did. This also shows the respondents that you value their efforts.

Think about the study objectives and how you might work in one of the following homework exercises.

# Homework examples

There are several types of homework assignments. Here are some more common ones and when you might want to use each.

## *Collage*

If a picture is worth a thousand words, a collage is, well, priceless. In this exercise, people combine pictures, drawings, photographs, words or objects together to make one collective thought. This exercise can help consumers articulate visually how they relate to a brand, product, or service in a way language alone cannot.

Having people create a collage at home can be easier than having them do it during the interview. At home, people have more time and more materials to draw from. This freedom can release their creative side and you may find you get better results. In the group or during the interview, ask the creator to talk about the collage. Have respondents walk through the images they chose to understand why they picked what they picked. Find out what the images, colors, and words represent to them. Don't assume that you know why Max put George Bush on his collage or why Linda picked an ocean scene. Wait and hear it in their own words. Listen to what they say and think about what that tells you about the brand or the category. A good wrap up question for collage discussion is to ask the creators to come up with a headline. This can sum up their feelings quickly and forces them to condense all the visuals into one idea or thought.

## Journal or diary

A diary is a written record of experiences and observations. Often diaries are used to increase a person's awareness of an event or experience. For example, in a study about a frozen dinner product, you might want to ask men to keep a journal at each meal. You may, for example ask them to record what they ate, when they ate, why they ate what they did, and how they were feeling. (If you worry about asking men to journal, tell them it is an event log.) This type of exercise helps people record their thoughts when they are in the moment. It is difficult, if not impossible, for someone to remember details of routine events that occur in the past. The diary can help people keep track of what they are doing and how they are feeling.

## Creative questions

Provocative questions can help the respondent get beyond tradition-ally functional or rational answers:

• What character or TV star do you feel like right now?

• What song comes to mind . . . ?

• If Brand X were a car, what kind of car would it be, and why?

• If you could have a do over right now, what would you what to change about this experience?

Like the collage, it is important to use the information from the diary during the interview. While you may not have time to discuss every entry during the interview, it is important to ask for highlights or inquire about key passages. To make the most of your interview time, try to review the diary ahead of time and be prepared with specific questions.

## Object to represent a feeling

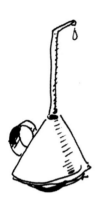

If you want to understand how people feel about something, ask them to find an object as a stand in. Think of this exercise as a 3-D metaphor. Here's how you might word the assignment: "Bring in an object that represents how you feel about the Delta SkyMiles program." or "Bring an object that represents how you feel about your favorite pair of jeans. And don't bring your jeans!" You can do a compare and contrast exercise in the same way by asking people to bring in two different objects to represent competing brands. For example: "Bring two objects, one that represents the Hilton and one that represents the Marriott."

The question should match the objective of the study. But this type of exercise can be helpful for understanding the relationship a person has to the category or a brand.

## Pictures

Having respondents take pictures while using your product, while shopping, or just as a simple way to show how they feel, can be a great way to get insight when you can't physically be with them. You can ask a mom to take pictures of her favorite meal made with your product. Ask her to take a picture of the inside of the refrigerator, the inside of the closet, or her office before and after she has cleaned her desk. Anything that you think will help you get closer to understanding the truth of her behavior.

## Questions to answer before you give homework

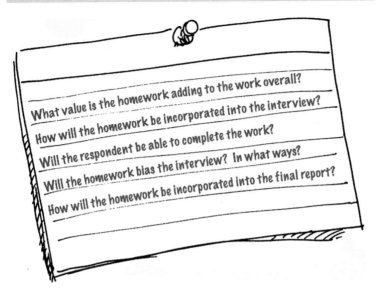

What value is the homework adding to the work overall?

How will the homework be incorporated into the interview?

Will the respondent be able to complete the work?

Will the homework bias the interview? In what ways?

How will the homework be incorporated into the final report?

## Homework setup

It is also important that the facility and the recruiters are aware of the assignment from the beginning. Homework not only impacts the incentive you need to pay but also the respondent cooperation rate. For incentives you should give everyone a homework honorarium. You can also consider a "best of" incentive for the one respondent who has the groups' favorite homework. (See Chapter 4 for more on incentives.) Homework also impacts the time you need to set aside to recruit. You will want to be sure that respondents have enough time between the time they are recruited to the time of the session to give the homework the proper attention.

When you draft the homework assignment, give careful thought to the instructions to be sure you get what you want. If you want poster-sized collages, say so. If you don't, say that too.

If you want stories that are at least three paragraphs long, say so. And if you want whatever they want to give you (and have a way to capture it, transport it, store it, and report it) say nothing.

When writing up the instructions, be sure the homework sounds like fun and not like a chore. You will get better results if you make it fun and creative from the beginning. Also, consider whether everyone needs to do the same exercise. You might instead invite respondents to choose among several options: ask them to tell a story, draw a picture, do a collage, or pick an object. This flexibility helps people work in the way in which they are most comfortable. Be sure you tell them that they cannot keep the assignment, unless of course they can. Generally the exercises are not returned but rather become part of the research archive—along with any video or audio recording from the interview.

## Incorporating homework into the report

Once you decide the assignment, consider how you are going to capture it for the report. Chances are that others besides those in attendance at the session will benefit from the work created by the respondents. The challenge can be conveying the pre-work effectively within the constraints of your report. Here are some ideas: scan images and create a scrap book with headlines and stories; take digital photos of the pre-work and include the images in the report; copy parts of the journal or dairy and create a composite diary of key passages; bring sample exercises with you when presenting results and place them around the room for people to see. Remember the goal is to bring the consumer to life as much as possible. Homework is a great way to do that!

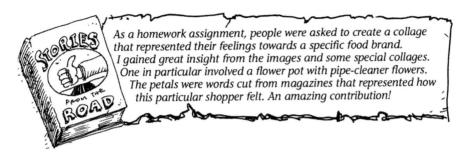

*As a homework assignment, people were asked to create a collage that represented their feelings towards a specific food brand. I gained great insight from the images and some special collages. One in particular involved a flower pot with pipe-cleaner flowers. The petals were words cut from magazines that represented how this particular shopper felt. An amazing contribution!*

## Exercises

Besides assigning homework to be done before the interview, you might want to use exercises during your interview. Exercises can be like a mental reboot. They can energize respondents and keep a group engaged. They can help you get to deeper insights that are only accessible when you move beyond the language barrier. For more on the science behind this, check out Gerald Zaltman's book, *How Customers Think: Essential Insights into the Mind of the Market.*

Here are some brief descriptions of exercises that you might want to try. Again, be sure you link the exercise to your objectives and don't think that the exercise takes the place of listening. You still need to talk about it why people did what they did.

### Mind map

Ask people to shout out top-of-mind associations with a brand or product. Record them on a flip chart as they are mentioned. The key is that people go with their first thought, rather than thinking it over. After you have captured all the words and phrases, review the flip chart and look for relationships between the items. This works best in a group setting, but be sure you can write quickly (and clearly) or you will be at a loss when it comes time to discuss the thoughts that were shared.

## Product sort

This works in groups and in individual interviews. The idea is to learn about how people view a category (for example) by giving them products and asking them to put them in groups according to some scheme that makes sense to them. After the sort is done, be sure you ask them to name each group.

## Image selection

Giving people a visual springboard can be a powerful tool for understanding all sorts of associations they have with brands and products. The exercise is simple. First, set out a large set of images, printed in color and on a heavy card stock when possible. Then ask people to select the one image that reminds them most of your brand, your product, etc. The rule, like most association exercises, is to encourage respondents to go with their gut. And the rule for pulling the picture set is to be metaphorical and symbolic, not literal and precise. For example, if your study were about automobiles, do not pull pictures of cars.

## Write before you speak

Sometimes you want to know about a person's first impression. That can be hard to do in a group setting. As soon as one person speaks, everyone else has been influenced. To eliminate that bias—to a degree anyway—give everyone a piece of paper and ask each person to write his or her first impressions down. Then when you go around the room they can speak from their notes. Always collect these sheets at the end of the session. It can be good to see what people wrote, in case it is different from what they said; and it just might be!

## *Thought bubbles*

Another way to get people to think out-of-the-box is to ask them to fill in thought bubbles above a fictional character's head. You might do a simple sketch of a woman pushing a shopping cart and ask people to write what she is thinking, feeling, or saying. This will give you insight into what your respondents are thinking, feeling, or saying, as people tend to project their own thoughts onto other people.

These are just a few examples and ideas. Have fun and your respondents will have fun too and you will learn more! "You learn more about a person in an hour of play than in a year of conversation." Or so said Plato.

# CHAPTER 11

# Groups: IDIs, Triads, and Dyads— oh my!

ONE of the first decisions you have to make is how many participants you want to include in the research session. This is as critical no matter whether you are going to a central location or to a person's home.

Groups are still the most common form of qualitative research. They can be creative and energetic, but they are often less likely to uncover emotional motivators and beliefs.

Thinking about your qualitative work in the past year, what percent of projects are from each of the following categories?

*Source*: 2010 Appleseed Survey of Researchers

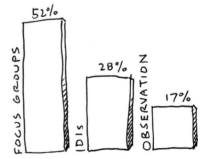

Let's start by stating the obvious. The number of people in a group is a function of two things, not equally weighted—project objective and cost. In the grand scheme of things 90 percent of the decision should be the objective and 10 percent of the decision should be the cost. Let's take the 10 percent first.

## Six of one, half-dozen of the other

Let's say that the average cost to do one standard six-person focus group is $2,400. Figure facility rental for two hours at about $300 and you get a per person cost of about $450. But, what if you wanted instead to do six one-on-one interviews? That would cost about $3,600 plus facility rental for a day at about $1,200. This scenario costs about $800 per respondent.

Now let's look at the "output" for each. If you assume equal participation, which is not a correct assumption but makes the math easy, a two-hour, six-person focus group yields about 12 minutes of output per person.

Compare that to the yield of 60 minutes per person in the case of the one-on-one interview. Add to that the value of having six individuals telling you what they think at a deeper level and not biased by other people's answers or simple presence and you start to see the value of the one-on-one model.

One six-person group = $2700 ($450 pp) ➡
　$42 per minute of output (max output = 12 minutes/pp)

Six one-on-one interviews = $4800 ($800 pp) ➡
　$13 per minute of output (max output = 60 minutes/pp)

However, this is only 10 percent of the story. The real story is not about the dollars, but the objective.

The key question you have to ask is this: what is the benefit of having people in a group versus talking to them one-on-one? My guess is that the more you ask that question up front, the fewer groups you will be doing.

I am not going to be one of the many who say focus groups are dead, but I do think you should be judicious in their use. The table below outlines the limitations of the group methodology versus the one-on-one methodology.

| One-on-One | Group |
|---|---|
| No group dynamic/team thinking and collaboration | Group think dynamic and collaboration |
| Bias is to the moderator but not to peers | Higher likelihood of socially acceptable answers |
| More individual input | Not all opinions expressed equally due to time or other constraints |
| Clearer top-of-mind insights | Limited top-of-mind insights |
| Deeper emotional insight | Collective emotion |
| I want consumers to tell me what they think, believe, or feel | I want consumers to interact and discuss a topic |
| Can be easier to schedule because of more available timeslots | Can be harder to schedule because groups are scheduled for specific time |
| Better for executive work | Good for brainstorming, creative, and collaborative sessions |
| Better for sensitive topics | |

## Group size

Once you have determined that you want to do groups and not individual interviews, the next question is how many people to invite. Some people will tell you to seat a focus group like you seat a dinner party, eight people, all pairs. Others prefer odd numbers so there are no "ties." Others might tell you they only seat six or that they like smaller groups of only three or four. There is no right answer. Research is an art as much as a science and nowhere is this more true than in qualitative work.

A few things are true. Most qualitative researchers would agree large groups can easily get unwieldy, and having fewer than three people (unless they know each other) can be uncomfortable for your respondents.

Dyads (two people) and triads (three people) are good when interviewing related subjects—like couples, families, friends, or classmates. People in these situations can share more, but may not feel they can speak openly as they are less anonymous. Smaller groups often yield more emotional findings and allow the moderator to probe responses more. Groups are best when you want to develop a collaborative environment and hear several people work through issues.

## Setups

Be sure you also consider how you want to set up the groups. Do you want to separate men from women? Do you want to separate married people from single people? Do you want to separate brand lovers from brand haters? These decisions can help you determine the right size for the session.

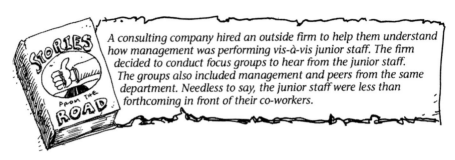

*A consulting company hired an outside firm to help them understand how management was performing vis-à-vis junior staff. The firm decided to conduct focus groups to hear from the junior staff. The groups also included management and peers from the same department. Needless to say, the junior staff were less than forthcoming in front of their co-workers.*

The last word:  You will notice I have not put **time** anywhere in this equation. Please do not be tempted to use time as a factor when making decisions like how many people to have in your research session. For example, thinking, "I can do 40 interviews in two days if I do groups but only 10 if I do one-on-one interviews" will get you into trouble. It is apples and oranges.

## Questions to ask to decide how to size your sessions.

What do I need to accomplish?
Is deep insight important?
Or group collaboration?
How sensitive is my topic?
What are my timing or budget constraints?

# CHAPTER 12

# Central Locations, On-Sites, In-Store, and Other Non-traditional Locations

THE MOST common way to execute research is to do it in a central location. In the Appleseed poll, researchers reported that 88 percent of the qualitative work they did in the past year was in a research facility.

On the plus side, groups in facilities are easy to conduct because they have the necessary infrastructure. The facility is set up to host groups easily. It has recording equipment and viewing rooms, test kitchens, comfortable waiting rooms, and check-in areas for participants, hostesses or hosts, and food options on-site and off. In addition, respondents are generally comfortable coming to an office-like setting in a public space.

On the negative side, some have been vocal about the use of central locations and how "contrived" they can be. Dev Patnaik of design strategy firm Jump Associates likens focus groups to ". . . a customer terrarium, with people behind glass—taken out of their natural surroundings and observed for scientific purposes . . ." Clearly this is not the effect we as researchers are trying to achieve, but, as my wise friend often says, "It is what it is." So we must work harder to overcome the terrarium effect to get to the truth.

Consider your objectives and you might reconsider your location. Whereas, on balance, using a facility will make your work so much easier, it may diminish your ability to get to real insights. In addition, you may find that on occasion your project requires you to travel to a location where there are no research facilities. Hard to imagine, but true. When the need arises, here are some ideas for non-traditional options for your interview or focus group.

## A change of space

**Hotel meeting rooms** Many hotels offer meeting-room space that is right sized for groups or interviews. If you go this route, be sure you think about where you are going to have people wait before the session starts and necessary on-site signage to direct people as they arrive.

**Restaurants, cafes or coffee shops** Based on the time of day, restaurants and the like might let you reserve space for free or for a small fee. And you get the added bonus of having food and drink available right on site.

**Public community spaces** Libraries, schools, and church basements may be available for a small fee or free. If you go this route, you will want to be sure you have thought through all the logistics for set-up, including seating, tables, video and audio equipment, signage, etc.

**Virtual office space** These offices cater to professionals who are on the road or work from home. Many also offer offices and conference rooms for rent on a short-term basis—a day or two.

**Corporate event facilities** Places that hold retreats often have different types of spaces that could be good options for your type of study.

## Go to the action

If you are interested in product insights, talking to people where they interact with the product can be far more valuable than bringing them out of the experience and into a facility. If you want to get into the mind and soul of your target audience, going to their homes for one hour will reveal more about them than two hours in a focus group room. If you want to know what your guests think of your theme park, go to the theme park. Going shopping with someone to experience what she experiences at the point of sale can get you closer to understanding your packaging, your competition, and how your brand plays out in the retail environment than any amount of time in a facility.

## Think like a repoter

Think of yourself as a reporter and not a researcher. Where would you go for the story? Who would you talk to? Challenge yourself to get out of the facility and go to where the action really is. But do it right. Be sure you have the proper authority to be where you are and that you are not trespassing. Have appropriate identification, have the necessary release forms for people to sign and any honoraria. Be courteous but tenacious, and you will get the interview.

If you reframe the question, and think instead about where you would hold a meeting, rather than where you would hold a focus group, you will certainly come up with many options. When using any of these non-traditional locations, be sure you get a sense of the space before you arrive to be sure it will suit your needs.

If you are doing work outside of a facility, you need to determine the best way for capturing the interview. Go to Chapter 15 for more on this.

# CHAPTER 13

# Maximizing the Facility Space

MOST PEOPLE today are at least moderately familiar with focus groups and what they are. Television programs from *The Simpsons* to the *Today Show* have featured focus groups, so the concept is more recognizable to the public. Even so, when you think about it, you are asking people to attend a fairly peculiar event. They are going to wait in a lobby until called, and then go into a 12-by-12 foot room with fluorescent lighting, a wall of mirrors, a microphone in the ceiling, a camera in the wall, and very little decoration except maybe, if you're lucky, a ficus in the corner. Not exactly a warm and welcoming feeling, right?

Add to this the fact that the respondents don't know each other, or you, or often the reasons why they are there. The moderator's first job is to put the respondents at ease and a comfortable facility space can play a big role. The space also needs to be conducive to the work. Think about whether you will have the space and the tools you need. More on that later, but first let's make the room more cozy.

I love the idea of natural light and so do most people. If you can pull it off, natural light is better than fluorescent in terms of video quality too. Your respondents will look healthier (no green pallor) and will be more energized with some sunlight in the room. This isn't always an option, but the next time you are in a facility, open the blinds! You might be surprised at the impact this small change has on the mood in the room.

Next, think about the table setup. Often you won't have a choice, but will have to work with the facility's furniture. But you might have some options. Ask yourself. Do I want a square table with all sides equal? A rectangular table with people on the ends? A circular table? A U-shape? No table at all? Think it doesn't matter? Of course, it does.

Think about the "power" dynamic you set up with the furniture. Having a table between the moderator and the participant is a different dynamic than having everyone sitting on couches and chairs with no barrier between them.

Think, too, about the dynamic you are setting up for the respondents. The Knights of the Round Table sat at a round table to show that all the knights were equal. Square or rectangular tables can create unintentional hierarchies. The head of the table is the power position and it goes from there. Research has also shown a direct relationship between distance and language; "the nearer a respondent is to an interviewer, the greater the number of words in the answers."* The goal is to maximize comfort, minimize hierarchy, and have everyone feel they can contribute to the discussion.

---

*Source: Raul Perez, Quirk's Marketing Research Review, May 2010*

## Square

Traditional and common, allows for good use of space, can be better for moderator-to-respondent eye contact, better for respondent-to-respondent eye contact, better for video and back room coverage, better for smaller groups—like six (two on each side), also good for dyad and triad groups if the table is smaller or more intimate, can be used to minimize interpersonal distance.

## Rectangle

Traditional and common, allows for a good deal of space for each person (usually), can eliminate the respondent power positions if you don't use the head of the table (opposite the moderator), okay for moderator-to-respondent eye contact, poor respondent-to-respondent eye contact, difficult for the back room to see all people (problem increases as the table gets longer), higher distance between the moderator and the people on the ends. This might lessen their engagement.

## Round

Somewhat common, gives respondents less area to work and the moderator less privacy, can aid eye contact all around (no pun intended), good for video and back room coverage, good for smaller groups (like 6) and larger groups (like 10), could be good for dyad or triad groups if the table is smaller and more intimate, will tend to minimize interpersonal distance, less power here (Knights of the Round Table), puts the group in "power."

## Half moon

Less traditional and less common than round tables, smaller work surface for respondents, great for moderator-to-respondent eye contact, less ideal for respondent-to-respondent eye contact, excellent for video and back room coverage, better for smaller groups, also good for dyad and triad groups if the table is smaller or more intimate, can minimize interpersonal distance, puts the moderator in "power."

## Classroom or U shape

Usually available upon request, but not common for traditional groups of 8 or fewer people. Better for larger groups, but creates a feeling of formality, which may inhibit the group's dynamic. Sets up the moderator as the authority.

## No table

Having no table at all is another trend in research. Rooms set up with couches and comfy chairs and coffee tables are being used more frequently. These room styles are believed to allow respondents to be more relaxed and more creative. Consider the respondent and the topic before deciding on this setup. If you or your respondents need space to set up material or to work, this room layout may not be your best bet. Ask for pictures to preview the furniture and the arrangement. Also, you would be wise to view the living room at the outset.

Having a table creates a natural but not awkward barrier between the respondent and the moderator, which can be comforting for some people. The table is like a podium; some people like to hide behind the podium, others like to be out in front.

*On a research trip we asked a facility to do a "living room" setup for us. We were interviewing couples, and thought a sofa would be more comfortable than a table and chairs. The day of the research arrived. We were discouraged to see that the sofa looked as if it had been through a flood, which the facility tried to hide by covering it with table cloths. It did not work. Plus, the camera angle in the room made the sofa look like an island unto itself! We decided to go back to the table setup rather than inviting our guests to sit on the dilapidated, table cloth sofa island. I could not imagine a good rapport in such a situation. Better to have your respondents be comfortable, feel welcome, and relaxed, than stick to your plan.*

## The last word: Size matters

Be sure when you set up your project that you discuss with the facility coordinator the size of the room you will need. If you are doing one-on-one interviews you do not want to be in a larger room and vice versa. It's like a wedding where half the seats are empty, or a party for 10 people in a closet. Awkward!

Be sure you ask about "right-sized" rooms up front so you don't find yourself squeezing 10 people in a space that's too small, or the opposite, talking to two people in a room with an echo!

Other things to consider: As part of the planning, be sure you also think about the things you may or may not want in the room with you. Here is a list of items for you to consider.

### Facility Check List

Flip charts
Easel / Wall Edge
Tacks for posting material
(ask first if it is OK)
White board
Dry erase markers
Side table(s)
TV/Video equipment
Internet / computer
Time keeper
Paper and pens

# CHAPTER 14

# Using Stimuli to Stimulate

CONSUMERS are people (a simple truth often overlooked). They are not robots or automatons, but human beings who can get distracted or bored talking about one topic for a long time. People want to tell you the truth but sometimes can't because they lack the right tools. Even if your study is the most interesting thing to you, and your product or ad or brand the most memorable, it probably isn't for everyone else in the room. People can be easily sidetracked by their own agendas.

This is just one of the reasons to use stimuli in a research interview. You can feel the change in the room where there is a prototype, an image, a video, or a song—anything that stimulates the senses. Stimuli can include a product prototype, a storyboard for an ad, or a set of images used to prompt a reaction from the respondent.

Here are some keys for using stimuli in research.

When possible, create and carry extra sets of your stimuli. Best practice is to bring more than one of everything. The more interviews you have planned, the more stimuli you should bring because the more things are handled, the more they will degrade.

This can be costly in the case of prototypes or mocked-up packaging, but it is generally worth it. If your stimulus is two dimensional or easily copied (like images, videos, music), there really is no excuse not to carry back up. If your stimulus is three dimensional or difficult to duplicate, consider a back-up method like a large image or cut out. If you are bringing samples, be sure you know that there is sufficient room for storage, including refrigeration if necessary.

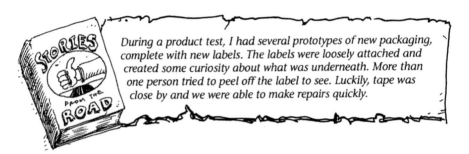

*During a product test, I had several prototypes of new packaging, complete with new labels. The labels were loosely attached and created some curiosity about what was underneath. More than one person tried to peel off the label to see. Luckily, tape was close by and we were able to make repairs quickly.*

## Bring a digital camera

When working with stimuli you may ask consumers to do an exercise, sorting products for example. The best and often easiest way to capture the work when it is done is to photograph it. A digital camera is best of course because the digital images can be stored electronically and imported into your final presentation, saving the effort of printing and scanning. This trick also works for capturing work done on flip charts and white boards either created with the client or with the respondent. Like carrying extra stimuli, it always pays to have extra memory, batteries, or the charger for the camera, just in case.

## Number and mark critical pieces of stimuli

Often research will require you to share confidential information with your respondents. While you should already have signed nondisclosure agreements, safeguarding material is still good practice. The easiest way to be sure that a top-secret idea does not end up in the wrong place is to number each piece. That way you can collect them at the end and be absolutely sure you are taking back everything you handed out in the beginning.

Instruct people that should they need to leave the room at any time, all material should be left at their place. That way you maintain more control over materials and don't have to worry about where Martha's concepts went or if Ricki took her notes with her.

To help people as they talk about stimulus material, assign each item a name, number, or letter. This helps respondents refer to specific material and also helps everyone in the back room keep track of what's happening (often they cannot see the same thing the respondent sees). Imagine four ad concepts. Rather than saying, "the one with the blue car and the blond woman," a respondent could say "Concept TH" and everyone would be on the same page.

## Labels matter

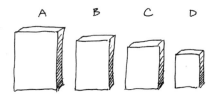

**Be sure** that your assignments do not suggest order. For example, if you have four ad concepts, using sequential numbers like 1, 2, 3, 4, or letters like A, B, C, D, can suggest a bias (even an unconscious one) that might influence the respondent.

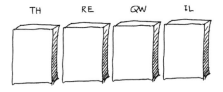

Use non-sequential markers like TH, RE, QW, IL. These can be meaningful (perhaps referencing a shorthand that you and the client understand) but should be generic enough that it would not influence the respondent.

## Back room tip

Put the concepts with their ID on a bulletin board in the back room or hand out packets to the observers. This will help people stay on track—if I had a dollar for every time I've heard, "Which concept is that?" It also can help the moderator if the same stimulus is going to be used more than once. The moderator can simply record the "code" and leave the material for the next group.

Another idea to consider is to develop your own set or sets of stimulus materials. This might include pictures for personification exercises, images for a sort, and brand logos for association. Having a set you use often can help cut down on prep time. Finding the right images and printing them can be time consuming. Better to do it once and do it well than to do it each time you are going out the door.

## Hints for using stimulus:

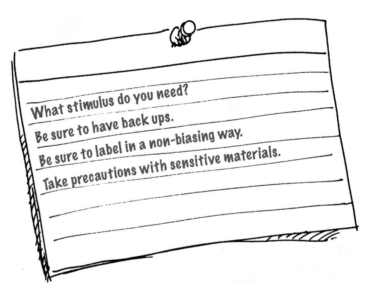

What stimulus do you need?

Be sure to have back ups.

Be sure to label in a non-biasing way.

Take precautions with sensitive materials.

# CHAPTER 15

# Capturing the Interview

WHEN planning research of any kind, it is always helpful to start with the end in mind. If you were making a birthday cake, you would think about what you wanted it to look like (what design, what size, what flavors, what colors) before you went out shopping for ingredients, right?

These questions will get you going:

What do you want to serve up at the end of this project?

How do you want to serve it?

## Getting good video

The cameras in any central facility are apt to take a pretty poor picture. Most are set up to do two things; first to shoot the entire room, and second to be inconspicuous.

While this makes sense in theory, in practice you can end up with grainy images where you can hardly tell who's talking!

To be more discreet, many facilities mount their cameras in the client viewing room and not in the interview room. So not only are you shooting from the ceiling using a fisheye lens, you are shooting through mirrored glass.

In addition to the variable video quality, the audio can be hard to understand. Again, in most cases, the microphone is mounted in the ceiling, and often picks up ambient noise (side conversations, papers rustling, people coughing, fluorescent lights humming) along with the actual discussion you want to record. This can make getting audio clips or written transcripts difficult.

This chapter deals with options for improving the quality of the video and audio from your research session.

## BYO

Bring your own camera and microphone. The quality of most camcorders today is superior to what you will encounter in many facilities. So spend a few hundred dollars and get a good camera with a nice, sturdy tripod and a good internal microphone and/or hook-ups for an external microphone. Some might argue having a camera in the room is obtrusive, but like the one-way mirror, within a few minutes, the respondents forget the camera. If you are doing any work outside a facility, chances are you will need your own camera equipment. While it is an investment, it will give you more flexibility and make your video more professional. To find the right solution, go to a reputable camera shop and tell them what you need. Places that specialize in photography and video can be more informative and helpful than big box stores. The web has lots of articles too and plenty of peer and professional reviews.

Having the right microphone (shotgun, wireless, or lavalier) is another consideration to be sure you are getting good audio to go along with your good video. Sophisticated options like wireless microphones can be more trouble than they are worth. Experiment with your equipment to determine if the camera's built-in microphone is sufficient, or if you need an external one.

Bottom line: invest in and use your own equipment as much as possible. When you use your own technology, you know what you are going to get and often you can get more professional looking video.

## Setting up equipment

Using your own equipment will require that you arrive far enough in advance of the first interview to get the equipment set up, to think about where to place the camera and how to frame the shots, and most importantly, to be sure everything is in working order. This doesn't need to take too long, but you will want to confirm with the facility that you will arrive early. That way, you can be sure the room will be open and available for your use.

While this may seem like extra work on your part—and you have enough to do already—it is worth it. The value of your work lies in your ability to bring the consumer insight to life for the client, the team, or the ad agency. Getting good images and audio is one step in making that happen.

## Other options

If you don't want to take the plunge into mini-movie making for research sake, tools like FocusVision and ActiviVision are available through facilities. These recording systems, set up ahead of time, digitize the interview and make it easy to create and download clips using online tools. In addition, they allow simulcasting to remote viewers. Be sure to plan for this up front. This type of equipment is not available at all locations and there are extra costs you will want to account for.

### Helping hands

If you film your own research, either at a central location or on site, you might also want to consider bringing a dedicated camera operator with you. This person can move the camera around the room to get the best shots. If you are using a system with a video marker tool (like FocusVision), assign someone (maybe your note taker) to mark the clips that are most interesting and relevant for the study.

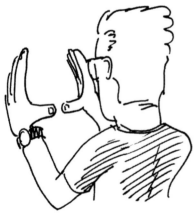

When you set up, frame the shot. Think about the background. Are you shooting a blank wall? Is there a plant coming out of your respondent's head? Have someone on the team stand in as a participant so you can frame the shot before respondents arrive. Move around and try to get a more interesting shot. This is especially important if you are doing one-on-one interviews in someone's home. The shot should tell the viewer something about the person.

Think about your light source. Are you getting the light from behind the person or from the front? The front is better. Back-lit shots can make the person appear as little more than a silhouette and you will have a hard time discerning their expressions if you can't see their faces.

Remember the rule of thirds for optimal person placement. Imagine the frame being divided into three equal sections horizontally and vertically. Place your focus where the lines intersect.

 Once you have framed the shot, give the respondent a marker so he or she knows exactly where to sit to stay in the shot. This can be as simple as a piece of masking tape on the floor or on the side of the table.

These tricks of the trade can help your research stand out and look more professional.

# SECTION 3

# Delivering the News

# CHAPTER 16

# Show Me, Don't Tell Me

TALKING to people is almost always interesting. If you don't agree, research might not be the right line of work for you. And, while general curiosity about people is a great attribute for a qualitative researcher, it is not enough. Market research, ultimately, is to inform action. If you don't understand what decisions are being made and how those decisions impact the business, your curiosity will ultimately leave you short. The value of the research will be measured in how much it helps the business make a decision, maybe today, maybe tomorrow, maybe months from now. All the work you have done up until now, is going to live forever in the report you create. Yet, in the 2010 Appleseed survey, 80 percent of those in the study said that reporting is an area in need of improvement. This rate is higher among mid-level researchers than senior research executives.

> *Help us do a better job of connecting learnings to broader issues. I feel like often we field a day of groups and the entire perspective is though the lens of those groups and nothing else is tied in. Have a better business sense.*

Source: 2010 Appleseed Survey of Researchers

Time and time again, I hear the same lament from clients, the research "fell short" because it had no context and had no recommendations for action. This is evident in the Appleseed Survey as well.

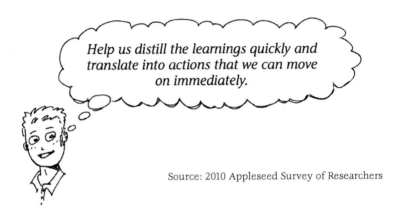

Source: 2010 Appleseed Survey of Researchers

These findings underscore the importance of having reports that show you understand the situation, the business, and the brand, most importantly so you can answer the "Now what?" question that is on everyone's mind. If you are the research supplier, ask questions of the client beyond the scope of the project; this will give you context for your work and you will immediately be working from a stronger foundation.

## Reporting

Next let's talk about how to make reports more actionable and more engaging. Ask yourself, "Who wants to know what and why?" Thinking about the *why* and the *who* will help you get to the *what*. Said another way, start with the end in mind. Why are you doing the research? Is the goal to a) inspire, b) educate, or c) decide? This answer will help you not only with the methodology and research plan but with the deliverable as well.

## 3 Destinations

If the goal is to **inspire**, your deliverable should be, well, inspirational; it should be visual, creative, and if possible multi-sensory.

If your goal is to **educate**, your deliverable should be informative and memorable. Education is lost if it is not remembered.

If your goal is to **decide**, your deliverable should start with the answer or the decision and provide a rationale for that recommendation.

For decision-based presentations and reports, look at the Minto Principle. This was first introduced in 1987 and offers a way to think about writing and problem solving using a pyramid structure. The premise is that the top of the pyramid is the answer to the key question. The building blocks underneath the apex are the support points to that apex. It is a great tool for organizing your report and for organizing your research. The book is called *The Minto Pyramid Principle: Logic in Writing, Thinking and Problem Solving* by Barbara Minto.

We also know that clients want reports that "speak" to them. The benefit of qualitative research over quantitative research is the dialogue. As researchers you have the chance to ask consumers questions, hear the answers, and ask more questions. You can listen to them talk with each other. You can spark new ideas from their ideas. You can listen! You can't say the same about quantitative studies, so why deliver reports like you would for a quantitative study? Why not help the reader, the client, the agency, the decision maker have the same experience you did in conducting the research? Clients want it. And you can give it to them. The next chapter will talk more about how to do this, but suffice it to say, research reports need to go further to satisfy the audience.

# CHAPTER 17

# Start Spreading the News . . .

Now that you have the input you need and the images and audio you want, you have a few options as to what to do with them. Let's think about good, better, best. *Good* is a written word report with quotes. *Better* embeds clips in a PowerPoint report. *Best* is to go beyond PowerPoint. For a quick read, check out the recently published book, *Real Leaders Don't Do PowerPoint* by Christopher Witt. You will find this a challenging and provocative read. For another quick read, check out Seth Godin's ebook, *Really Bad Powerpoint (and how to avoid it)*. It is a great use of a spare 15 minutes!

Don't just take my word for it. The 2010 Appleseed Survey of Researchers says that the second most critical area for improvement is "telling the story." In fact, more than three in four researchers want this to be better.

So how can you tell a better story? How can you get your audience to experience the consumer first hand?

The challenge is that research is not always "presented." Rather, it is often delivered in an email or as a document. In addition, when research is presented, it is not always the case that it is visually engaging.

## Recall

At the 2010 Brandworks Conference in Madison, On Your Feet presented a compelling statistic: most of us (when not under stress) will recall about 30 percent of what we see and about 20 percent of what we hear. Under stress, these percentages are lower. But we recall about 50 percent of what we see *and* hear.

None of this is that surprising. We are hard wired as human beings to learn through stories. We all know the story of "The Boy who Cried Wolf." We know what it means when someone says we are acting like a Cinderella. We learn these stories as children because they teach us lessons and they stay with us. Each of us can remember these characters and these stories because they engage the creative side of our brain. But I doubt that many of us can remember the presentation we heard last month. Data doesn't stay with us as long as stories do.

## Pop Quiz!

**What is the license plate number from your first car?**

**What will you tell your grandchildren about what happened on September 11, 2001?**

Stories are accessible; data is not. However, data in the form of a story works. As a researcher, it can help to think as a storyteller rather than as a researcher. When you tie data together into a cohesive story your work will be more memorable. If you arrive at a "moral" for the story, your work will be more actionable. If

you present it in a visual way, it will stay with people longer.

I advocate that best practice is to create a video report when you can, rather than a report with video in it. And this notion is echoed in the sentiment expressed in the Appleseed Survey:

*Improved multi-media reporting to bring the consumer and learnings from the project "to life."*

Source: 2010 Appleseed Survey of Researchers

This can be easy to do using readily available movie-making software programs. Final Cut and iMovie are powerful and very user friendly. PC programs like Adobe Premier can also be used to create video reports. Once you have your video created, it can be burned to CD/DVD and become self-contained consumer stories easily shared and understood.

# CHAPTER 18

# Moving Interviews Online: Everyone's Doing It

TODAY, qualitative research is not just about doing in-person interviews, home visits, or shop-alongs. It is about connecting to people where they connect with people—namely the Internet.

Over the past 10 years or so, a plethora of web-based tools have become available to help qualitative researchers extend their reach beyond the facility and beyond the in-person study. While nothing will ever replace the opportunity (and the privilege) to talk with someone face to face, online tools certainly have a place in qualitative research. Like everything else, the research method you use needs to be balanced against the project goals, objectives, and logistical constraints, like time and money.

Online qualitative is used because it offers some benefits that in-person qualitative does not. Online qualitative is everywhere there is Internet so you are not constrained by location. Often this is a strong selling point because it allows researchers to have a broader reach without racking up frequent flier miles.

Online qualitative also provides for more privacy. Even in the case of one-on-one interviews respondents might be shy about opening up and sharing personal experiences. The Internet offers another level of anonymity that might allow for deeper sharing.

Online qualitative is often asynchronous. This means that rather than inviting people to a group or interview on a specific date and time, they are invited to participate over several days at their leisure. This flexibility can be critical depending on your audience. In addition, online qualitative is typically not limited to a finite window of time like traditional interviews. Whereas a focus group might last two hours, or an individual interview 45 minutes, online qualitative may take place over several days. This allows the respondent time to think about questions or to complete exercises.

Here are some of the more common online research tools and when you might consider using each.

## Bulletin boards

Bulletin boards are set up to feed respondents questions at pre-set, regular intervals and to invite discussion among the board participants. Typically lasting several days or more, boards are the most common type of online qualitative research. Bulletin boards are quite flexible and include direct questions, stimuli for reaction such as words, video, or images, and even assignments, such as "go to Store X and shop for this product." Bulletin boards often have more participants than a typical focus group. But having too many can inhibit the discussion and your ability to guide the flow. If you decide a bulletin board is the route for you, be sure you give careful consideration to the setup, including how you will recruit for each, how you will feed questions to the board and at what intervals, and how the board will be moderated to guide discussion. Remember that you might start with 25 people, but lose some along the way.

At the end of the bulletin board you can expect, at a minimum, to get transcripts of the discussion. You may also have access to online tools to help you mine the rich volume of data collected. Depending on the supplier you work with to set up or host the bulletin board, you might also get a report.

## Online focus groups

Unlike the asynchronous bulletin board, the online focus group is real time and lasts at most a few hours, rather than several days. These can be text or audio/video based. Tools like Skype have made video chatting much more accessible. Online focus groups can be very useful when trying to set up a discussion among a low-incidence population because geography is taken out of the equation.

Just like any qualitative method, you will want to be sure that respondents are engaged in the process. This can be harder when your work is online, because you aren't in the room and therefore can't see body language. Be sure you think about the flow of the discussion guide and how you might incorporate exercises to keep the momentum going. Also, be careful not to pack too much into the session. If the group goes too long, you are likely to get people dropping out. Think about yourself sitting in front of a computer for more than an hour or so and you start to get the picture.

## Other considerations

The tools available to online researchers grow every day, and before you settle on a supplier or a methodology, it is wise to review the options available and ask yourself what will work for your study.

**Online research tools to think about:**

words or pictures

diaries or journals

webcams

collage tools

editing tools

"back-room" tools

transcripts

analytic tools

panel

dashboards

mark-up tools

# APPENDIX A

# Glossary of Marketing Research Terms

*Asynchronous*: Most commonly used in reference to online qualitative. Asynchronous research is research that occurs over time, rather than at a specific time.

*Central Location Test* (CLT): Refers to research done at a central location like a focus group facility.

*Concept*: An expression of an idea for the purpose of consumer testing. Concepts could include ad concepts, message ideas, or product concepts. Concepts (unlike prototypes) are typically rough expressions in two-dimensional form—like an ad storyboard for example.

*Discussion Guide*: The interview guide used by the moderator to lead the research session.

*Dyad*: A focus group with two participants.

*Ethnography*: An observational study, which typically takes place in a participant's home or in an experiential setting (like a store, park, event).

*Floater*: A person recruited to be on hand as backup in case of a no show. Floaters must meet the study criteria and are asked to be in the facility or on call for a longer period of time than a regular respondent.

*Focus Group:* A research event that typically includes between 6 and 8 people.

*Incidence:* The percent of people who are expected to qualify for the study.

*In-Depth Interview* (IDI): Typically a lengthier interview designed to get deeper information from a respondent. These are generally done one-on-one and last a few hours.

*Intercept:* A method for recruiting participants. An intercept study "intercepts" people at a public location and qualifies and invites them to participate in the research. Malls are common intercept locations.

*Moderator:* The person or persons who facilitate the research either by leading the focus group, the interview or the observation. The moderator is often the person responsible for writing the report.

*One-on-One Interview:* Any interview with just a moderator and a participant. Not all one-on-ones are in-depth interviews.

*Online Qualitative:* A term that refers to a growing number of techniques such as online focus groups, bulletin boards, and chat rooms, available for conducting qualitative research online.

*Panel:* A set of people who have agreed to be contacted for research purposes. Panels are managed by research facilities and by panel companies.

*Product Placement:* Sending a product out to a consumer for use before the research. You are "placing" the product with them for a test drive.

*Projective Techniques:* A set of techniques with roots in psychology designed to elicit responses from the unconscious mind.

*Prototype:* An example of a product. Prototypes are typically three-dimensional and may or may not be fully functional.

*Recruitment Grid*: A summary (usually in spreadsheet form) that lists the participants for a study and key data about them, including demographics and participation criteria.

*Screener*: Participant criteria in the form of a questionnaire such that it can be used to recruit for specific research studies.

*Stimuli*: Anything that participants can interact with or react to in a research setting. Stimuli could include photos, ads, prototypes, or sounds.

*Triad*: A focus group with three participants.

# APPENDIX B

# Tools You Can Use – Right Now!

## Innovations in—

### Recording interviews

**Digital note pens.** These nifty little devices can help your project move along more efficiently. There are two basic types: pens that digitally store your handwritten notes and pens that record audio. The Livescribe pen can do both. Reviews have been mixed on these pens, but with a little research you can find something to suit your needs. Be sure you check and see if you need special paper (which can get expensive) and of course that the software is compatible with your computer.

### Web-based file sharing programs

For people who do not have access to an FTP server, there is a tool called **YouSendIt** (*www.yousendit.com*) which makes sharing large files a breeze. Simply upload the material you want to send and off it goes. At the time of this writing, you can send files up to 100 MB for free. Fees for larger files are minimal. The site offers security features that you should certainly check out.

If you have a Mac, consider MobileMe not only for the flexibility it allows in general file storage and integration, but also because of the file-sharing feature. If you want to share a file, you can easily send a secure link and password for people to access. The fees for MobileMe are based on an annual subscription and are relatively inexpensive.

### Video taping interviews and consumer experiences

Flip video cameras are handy, compact, easy-to-use and can be helpful in a variety of ways. They are a good option if you don't want to get a high-end camera, and can be an inexpensive way to get video from consumers, too. Consider sending them out to respondents and asking them to take video as part of a pre-work assignment. Prices start at around $150 and features include high-definition video (HD) and several hours of recording time.

### Summarizing text data

Word Clouds. If you do qualitative research for any amount of time, you are likely to be exposed to "automated" tools for text analysis. Some of the more interesting and visual tools available are those that create word clouds. Word clouds take an abundance of words and make them visual; the more often a word comes up, the bigger it appears in the cloud. Words that are used less often appear smaller. Pretty straightforward. Here is an example. This is a summary of what people in the 2010 Appleseed Survey of Researchers said when asked about what could be improved with qualitative research.

drivers
learning summary
problems business
process Provide content
effective highlights
articulate insightful addressed
sit Communicate lead interviews
interaction respondent objectives
Recruit action enthusiastic arise
emotional reports group relative
respect opportunity necessarily fix
executive results

www.tagxedo.com

This particular word cloud was created using one of the several web-based tools for creating word clouds—Tagxedo.com. You too might find this tool useful in summarizing results.

### Video chat

Today video chat is readily available using tools like Skype. Faster Internet connections and built-in video cameras have made it easy to see and talk to people. Skype is also useful as a way to present results when you can't be there in person.

## Good Tools—

### Meeting management

*Doodle.com.* Finding a time that everyone can meet can be one of the more frustrating things in planning qualitative research. Doodle, a free online tool, allows people to find common times. Check it out next time you have a meeting to schedule or an event to plan.

### Online qualitative

*Wordpress.org.* If you decide to go the online qualitative route, you may want to develop your own blog space for discussions with respondents. Wordpress.org lets you build your own "blog" for use with qualitative.

# APPENDIX C

# Project Checklist

Use this list to be sure you have crossed all the t's and dotted all the i's for your next project. Times are estimates.

| | |
|---|---|
| **Right away** | Determine objectives and research plan |
| **Three weeks** | Schedule facility (if needed) |
| | Schedule / retain moderator (if needed) |
| | Finalize participation criteria |
| **Two weeks** | Finalize recruitment plan (including recontacts) |
| **One week** | Confirm facility needs (AV/remote viewing etc.) |
| | Finalize the moderator discussion guide |
| | Prepare and label stimuli |
| | Prepare any material for exercises |
| | Confidentiality / Release forms |
| **Two days ahead** | Send incentives to facility |
| **Day of** | Re-screen participants |
| | Double-check setup and technology |
| | Set up back room for viewers (including final recruitment grids, discussion guide, and stimuli) |

# Index

# About the Author

 **Mary Kathryn Malone** began her career in journalism in 1992, and has never stopped being curious about people. Over the past two decades she has been a producer, a statistician, a moderator and a teacher—often wearing more than one hat at a time! Her work has helped companies launch new products, attract new customers, develop killer ads, and build stronger brands.

Mary K. is a generalist and has worked in a variety of industries: consumer products, higher education, healthcare and leisure, but she has deep experience on which to draw, making her the perfect research partner.

In addition to all things research, Mary K. makes it a point to give back. She has served as a member of the External Advisory Board of the A.C. Nielsen Center, volunteers on the Vision5K marketing committee, helps grant wishes for the Make-A-Wish Foundation, and runs marketing workshops for entrepreneurial women at the Center for Women and Enterprise.

Mary K. earned an MBA from the University of Wisconsin-Madison where she was an A.C. Nielsen Research Scholar. She is a member of several professional groups and regularly participates in seminars and trainings at many of the research industry's leading organizations.

To reach Mary K. directly: *maryk@appleseedci.com*

# About the Illustrator

**Mike Thomas** is a creative director with 18 years experience in brand and licensing design. After graduating with a degree in communications design from Pratt Institute, Mike joined Marvel Enterprises as an art director. He was soon promoted to creative director and worked on properties like *Spider-Man the Animated Series, The Incredible Hulk,* and *X-Men,* the movie. With Chris Dickey, he founded Creative Giant in 2001. He can be reached at *mthomas@creativeGIANT.net.*